HOME FOR THE HOMILY
The Sacred Art of Homiletics

Kiki Latimer

En Route Books and Media, LLC
Saint Louis, Missouri

⊕ENROUTE

Make the time

En Route Books and Media, LLC

5705 Rhodes Avenue

St. Louis, MO 63109

Contact us at contactus@enroutebooksandmedia.com

Cover credit: Katie Latimer

© 2022 Kiki Latimer

ISBN-13: 978-1-956715-41-5

Library of Congress Control Number: 2022935625

Kiki Latimer is available for booking!

Kiki Latimer is available for speaking engagements, group workshops, private coaching, homiletic consulting, and educational seminars.

Contact her on her website www.kikilatimer.com or via email kikiwordworks@hotmail.com.

Dedicated to my first teachers of the spoken word
My beloved parents
Svend and Marguerita Munck

The Author has produced a Homiletic Masterpiece, theologically sound and pastorally relevant for seminarians, Seminary formators and the ecclesial audience. Highly recommended.

-Fr. Dominic Anaeto, Professor of Pastoral Theology, Holy Apostles College & Seminary, CT

I've known Kiki for many years and been a glad recipient of her Homiletics instruction. She offers important technical and practical insights to delivering God's Word to the faithful, which has been invaluable. I wholeheartedly recommend her work.

- Fr. Skip Thompson, MSA, Retreat Director, Santa Clara Parish, Oxnard, CA

I've been blessed to work with Kiki. Her guidance is simple, profound, and practical and deeply grounded in the Church's homiletic tradition. I recommend her wisdom to both veteran homilists and preachers in initial formation. She has made a tremendous contribution to the preaching of the Church.

-Fr. Erik Lenhart, OFM Cap. S.T.L. St. Lawrence Friary, Beacon, NY

Kiki Latimer's book is full of pungent insights into how priests should preach homilies. The fruit of years of teaching homiletics, I wish every seminarian, deacon and priest would read her book.

-Dr. Ronda Chervin, retired philosophy professor, author of numerous books about Catholic Spirituality, and media presenter.

Table of Contents

In Gratitude

Many people helped make this book possible. I am deeply grateful to the late Winifred Caldwell my original speech professor in the oral interpretation of literature, and beloved friend at the University of Rhode Island. I give special thanks to the Very Rev. Douglas Mosey, C.S.B., who as President-Rector of Holy Apostles College & Seminary opened for me the doors to teaching there; to Fr. Dominic Anaeto who welcomed me into his homiletics class, taught me so much, and reviewed the *Home for the Homily* manuscript; to Fr. Erik Lenhart and Fr. Ed Przygocki, M.S.A., who were a joy to work with in homiletics.

I am thankful to my dear friends Dr. Ronda Chervin and Fr. Dennis Kieton who also read the manuscript and gave innumerable great suggestions. My heart is forever grateful to the women religious, seminarians, deacons, and priests of Holy Apostles who graced my time with them and taught me perhaps far more than I taught them; their ideas, hopes, and struggles are contained herein.

I am thankful as well to the lay students, administration, and staff who became dear friends and made my time at Holy Apostles very joyful. I would like to especially mention my sweet buddy, the late Mary Welsh; together we shared the warmth of friendship over many a meal, as well as the warmth of her well-heated mail cubby on cold New England winter days.

My stay at Holy Apostles was made particularly possible by the generous and loving family that housed and homed me during my weekly overnights in Cromwell, Barbara and Andrew O'Keefe and their little dog Mitzi. They welcomed me into their lovely home on the Connecticut River where we shared meals, philosophical and theological discussions, life stories, and our faith. I consider my time and friendship with Barb and Andy one of the greatest blessings of my life.

To my dearest friend, colleague, and mentor, philosophy professor Dr. Stephen Schwarz, I give thanks for our many hours of philosophical, theological, and writing discussions that have spanned over forty years, and to his dear wife Sherry Schwarz who has blessed our friendship.

Most of all, my deepest appreciation to my loving husband Jim Latimer, who has always encouraged me, especially during this difficult pandemic year of writing. I give thanks to him and to our four adult children and thirteen grandchildren, who continue to give me an intimate and realistic view of how the homily is lived out in the domestic church.

Preface

It was in the Spring semester of 2014 that I was graciously invited by my dearest friend, colleague, co-author, and mentor, philosophy professor Stephen D. Schwarz to accompany him to Holy Apostles College & Seminary. We were there to discuss our book *Understanding Abortion* in the philosophy class of his life-long friend philosophy Professor Ronda Chervin. Fr. Douglas Mosey, C.S.B., the Rector of Holy Apostles, joined us that evening at the dinner table in the refectory. Over the course of dinner, Fr. Mosey invited me to return in the fall semester and give my ten-hour seminar on *Understanding Abortion* for the entire seminary and college.

It was during this week-long stay at Holy Apostles in the fall of 2014 that I was asked one afternoon, along with Ronda, to join in on a homiletics course given by Fr. Dominic Anaeto. Fr. Dominic needed an audience willing to listen to and comment on his seminarians' practice homilies. My educational background in the Oral Interpretation of Literature and years of coaching storytellers and speakers immediately came to life listening to these practice homilies. Several months later I wrote to Fr. Mosey and asked him for the part time position of privately coaching homiletics. I am deeply grateful for his affirmative response and subsequent support of my homiletic and educational endeavors.

After a short time, I became assistant to Fr. Dominic and began to learn the intricate rubrics of homily. I am deeply grateful to Fr. Dominic for taking me under his wing despite all our initial differences. We began as an odd couple of priest-layperson, man-woman, Nigerian-American, black-white, but we quickly found common ground in our very similar sense of humor, becoming not only colleagues, but good and lifelong friends.

From there I went on during the subsequent five years to assist several other priests, including Fr Erik Lenhart and Fr. Edward Przygocki, M.S.A., eventually teaching homiletics on my own, until the Covid-19 pandemic arrived in 2020. During my five years at Holy Apostles, I received my MA from Holy Apostles in Moral Theology. This enhanced my teaching of homiletics and complimented my twenty years of co-leading a Summa Theologica Study Group in Providence, RI, as well as my background in Ethics, Virtue Ethics, Metaphysics, Philosophy of the Person, and Epistemology.

Home for the Homily: The Sacred Art of Homiletics is the culmination of my education in the Oral Interpretation of Literature, Psychology, and Philosophy from the University of Rhode Island, philosophy teaching, my private speech coaching, and my years teaching and coaching homiletics at Holy Apostles. During my time at the University of Rhode Island, the Philosophy Department was unusually and predominantly Catholic and instrumental in both my education and conversion to the Church in 1985.

Thanks to Fr Mosey, who has since retired, the campus of Holy Apostles was, during my five years there, very open and welcoming of children. Therefore, I was often able to bring my grandsons to the campus where they were able to attend Mass, play ping pong, eat in the refectory, and interact on a regular basis with priests, seminarians, deacons, and religious sisters in a healthy and happy educational environment conducive to attracting young men to the priesthood. I think fondly on my youngest grandson, who at age four, was already asking if he too could go to "Holy Opossums!"

It is with great love that I look back on those five years of teaching some truly holy men both before and after they were ordained priests or permanent deacons, as well as coaching the resident Vietnamese religious sisters in public speaking.

These two years of pandemic isolation have allowed me time to write *Home for the Homily: The Sacred Art of Homiletics*, the written version of all that I both learned and taught in the classroom, in hopes of reaching a wider community. While rarely is any learning environment as wonderful as the educational setting of the actual classroom, it is my hope that I have here captured some of the essence of that experience for those in need of homiletic enrichment, improvement, and expansion as they speak the word of God in the Mass to the people of God. While this book has been written primarily for homiletic use by priests and deacons, many of the concepts contained herein may certainly be applied to many

public speaking engagements by those in religious life, as
well as by the laity in mission and evangelization leadership
roles.

Home for the Homily concerns a new and required depth
of preaching the word of God within the Mass. This calls for
a new and deeper appreciation of communication skills. The
homilist may no longer stand separately on the shoreline nor
drift in the safety of shallow waters; rather, he must have the
faith of Peter to "put out into deep water."[1] This requires
depth of soul, depth of character, depth of vulnerability, and
depth of skill. When Christ asks Peter to "put out into the
deep water,"[2] Peter considers his level of faith in Jesus and
decides, by grace, to do so. This is a pivotal moment; without
this affirmative decision there will be no catch. It is no different for the homilist today. The intimacy and depth of the
effective homily requires an affirmative decision to put out
into the deep. Notice that Peter refers to Jesus as "Master"[3]
when he is told to put out into the deep and lower the nets
for a catch. This is a level of intimate faith that demands that
the homilist know Who is the Master. Furthermore, note
that Peter has the skills necessary to put out into the deep.
Peter is able to put out into the deep due to his sincere faith,
tender submission, and essential skills. May *Home for the*

---

[1] NRSVCE, John 5:4
[2] NRSVCE, John 5:4.
[3] NRSVCE, John 5:5.

Homily: The Sacred Art of Homiletics help you, the homilist, put out into the deep and thereby, allow the homily to reach its four sequential destinations: the home of the Mass, the home of the Intellect, the home of the Heart, and the home of the Will, the domestic Church where the homily is lived out.

Foreword

The first transcendental imperative is to be attentive. However, it is one of the most difficult things to do. The primary element of the evangelical counsel of obedience is the ability to be attentive, to listen, to see, to feel, in such a manner as to be in intimate relationship - whether professional or personal. The more in our lifetime that we are not listened to, the less likely we are to speak. There is an interesting relationship between listening and speaking. If I have been listened to when I speak, the chances are that I will believe that other people will listen to me, as well.

I have known Kiki over the years as an attentive listener. The first time she sat in my Homiletics class, she was obviously fully immersed in the lecture: taking notes, asking profound questions, and making insightful contributions. I never suspected she had in mind to be greater than her professor, but that should be the joy of every professor, and that is sincerely my joy. She has garnished the notes she took with her skills in storytelling and poetry and in her being an attentive lay faithful in the ecclesial audience. She knows the difference between homilies that put an audience to sleep and a lively homily that is sensitive to the audience, challenging, uplifting, edifying, motivating, giving rise to fresh resolve and devotion.

Kiki presents herself in this book as an accomplished professor possessing the skill of communicating intricate and profound concepts and materials in a very simple manner that is easily digestible to the intellect and the heart. She conveys difficult themes in the nicest language, coating what can be the bitter pill with sweet tasting flavors.

In the pages of her book, Kiki has made an immense contribution to homiletic preaching: drawing principally from her giftedness as an attentive listener to homilies as well her impressive skills as a teacher of homiletic preaching in seminaries over the years. As a supremely accomplished storyteller, she has weaved the stories of divinity and humanity in a simple and digestible style.

In her book *Home for the Homily*, she eloquently demonstrates that a homily is all about presenting the word of God in a manner tailored to the audience sitting before the homilist, meaning that even a great homily may be addressed to the wrong audience. The effectiveness of the homily comes from using the word of God to address the contemporary needs of the people of God in the church – at that moment.

As one of the best ways of defining a concept is saying what it is not, Kiki has dealt in a comprehensive way on what a homily is not so as to help us better understand what a homily is. To make the homily homing, she suggests that the homilist begin with the beauty of goodness, transition to the radiance of goodness, and ultimately arrive at the clarity of the Truth of the good news. Going the opposite direction will make the shining light of the homily too dazzling for the audience, to the point of their easily giving up. It only takes a few seconds to either hold the audience in rapt attention or lose them completely.

Kiki doesn't mince words in emphasizing the Christocentric nature of homily. Preachers need to be heedful of the tendencies to preach about oneself or to simply entertain the audience. Homiletics is a sacred art! So, clarity of thought and precision in the choice of words employed should be the key to an effective homily delivery. Stories may play an essential role in the delivery of a homily, but a story must not be the feature of the homily. Rather, a story should be a supportive footnote to the body of the homily. The effective use of repetition and question will also lead an audience to internalize a homilist's message and retain it.

Because human beings are embodied beings, a homilist's body language actually can speak louder than the words he uses. Voice tone and inflection help to keep an audience alert and attentive. But, there is also power in the use of silence. Silence plays an indispensable, almost mystical role by allowing words to simmer for a moment in the heart of the audience. The homilist should be mindful that how he begins and ends his homily can either make or mar what otherwise is a beautifully crafted homily. Hence, even if committing an entire homily to memory is difficult, it is best to strive to memorize at least the beginning and end of the homily so as to avoid multiple endings that might confuse the audience.

I highly recommend Kiki's book for all who are seeking the clearest way of communicating and listening to the good news in any ecclesial setting. This easy-reading book is a special, and valuable, tool for seminary formators (educators), for seminarians preparing for the Catholic priesthood, and for priests and deacons desiring to improve their homiletic skills.

Rev. Fr. Dominic Anaeto, STL, STD
Professor of Pastoral Theology

Homily

Homily finds its ancient roots in the Greek *homilos,* meaning a crowd or a gathering. Greeks used *homilos* to create the verb *homilein* meaning to address the people, as well as the noun *homilia* meaning a conversation. Latin speakers graciously borrowed *homilia,* and then passed it on to Anglo-French. The spelling had changed to *omelie* by the time it meandered into Middle English, but by the mid-16th century the term had recovered the "h" and the "y" of its present day spelling.[1]

---

[1] https://www.merriam-webster.com/dictionary/homily#synonyms

Chapter 1

Homing the Homily

Bringing the Homily Home

The Homily seeks a home in the depth of the human heart. Home is where one belongs. Home is where one grows. Home is where one establishes both deep roots as well as wings. Everyone and everything need a home. Often, we may move from home to home, hoping never to be homeless in between. When home is missing, we use sorrowful words like homeless, displaced, refuged, destitute, itinerant, no-where to lay one's head. When everything has its home, its place in the universe, there is then the possibility of order, where goodness, beauty, and truth can thrive. The birds have their nests, foxes their dens, even our coffee cup has the cupboard. So, too, the Homily needs its home. The home for the homily begins first with its proper place within the Mass; it is then, secondly, moved to the home of our minds, and then, hopefully, thirdly, taken home to our domestic church, the home of our hearts and lives, as it is lived out in the will. This is the Church as *the home of the word.*[1] If this progression

---

[1] *Verbum Domini*, 181.

of home does not happen properly, the homily becomes homeless, lost in space, sound vibrations moving ever outward, destitute, nowhere to lay its head.

The homily, like the Eucharist, is meant to strengthen and nourish us beyond the home of the Mass. Unfortunately, all too often the homily does not make it out of the church doors. By the time we shake Father's hand, most of us would often be hard pressed to give even a basic account of the homily. Even if we remember what the homily was about, we have often been offered no ways in which to incorporate it into our daily lives. It remains an abstract blur of information detached from concrete formation and inspiration; it never entered the home of the intellect.

This book is about a deep and developed understanding of the tools necessary for an effective homily. The tripod of **information, formation,** and **inspiration** needed for a dynamic homily comes from both your lived cooperation with the Holy Spirit and a learned skill set. This is the homily that can be actually internalized from the home of the Mass to the home of the Intellect to the home of the Heart, such that it can be a source of inspiration and thereby implemented in our daily life. Why does it need to be brought home to the Heart? This third home leads to the final home of the homily, the Will. Here is the little church, the domestic microcosm of the Church, the basic unit of both the Church and society is in the heart of the family and community in which the individual acts. So, it is imperative that the homily makes it to the home of the heart which connects it to the home of the Will where it may reach fulfillment in action, in works.

The Home of the Homily within the Mass

The Mass is composed of two primary parts, the Liturgy of the Word and the Liturgy of the Eucharist. Even though the homily is technically part of the Liturgy of the Word, it acts as a sacred space, a covered bridge, between the two parts. Every good homily therefore points both back to what was just given in the readings (primarily the Gospel) and forward to our reception of the Our Lord Jesus Christ in the Blessed Sacrament. It is important to remember this job or vocation, so to speak, of the homily as a sacred covered bridge. It is a good image to bear in mind when composing a homily. If it does not reach clearly to the word, it will fall short; if it does not in some way connect with the Eucharist, it will fall short. Therefore, the homilist must stretch to do this job, and the homily must have clear supports to hold up under the pressure of its purpose. This is always, first and foremost, an act of co-creation and cooperation with the Holy Spirit.

The homily is first and foremost an *act of love* within the Great Act of Love of the Mass. "Through this revelation, therefore, the invisible God out of the abundance of His love speaks to men as friends and lives among them so that He may invite and take them into fellowship with Himself. This plan of revelation is realized by deeds and words having an inner unity."[2] We preach the Person of Jesus, the Incarnate Love of God. "Indeed, sharing in the life of God, a Trinity of love, is *complete joy*. And it is the Church's gift and unescapable duty to communicate that joy, born of an encounter with the person of Christ, the Word of God in our midst. In a world which often feels that God is superfluous or extraneous, we confess with Peter that he alone has 'the words of eternal life'. There is no greater priority than this: to enable the people of our time once more to encounter God, the God who speaks to us and shares his love so that we might have life in abundance."[3] The homilist must reflect this love through the homily, as well in the rest of his life. "If I speak in the tongues of mortals and of angels, but do not have love, I am a noisy gong or a clanging cymbal."[4] There are therefore three aspects of love that must always be conveyed in one way or another in the homily:

1) God really and truly loves us and invites us to love Him in return.

2) The Homilist loves God and wishes to share this relationship with us.

3) The Homilist loves us and personally cares about us.

---

[2] *Dei Verbum*, 2.

[3] *Verbum Domini*, 2.

[4] I Corinthians 13:1, NRSVCE.

"A good homilist, for example, is able to articulate the mystery of the Incarnation—that the eternal Son of God came to dwell among us as man—in such a manner that his listeners are able to understand more deeply the beauty and truth of this mystery and to see its connections with daily life. By highlighting his humanity, his poverty, his compassion, his forthrightness, and his suffering and Death, an effective homily would show the faithful just how much the Son of God loved them in taking our flesh upon himself."[5] When these aspects of love are implicitly or explicitly in the homily, the homily is on track. The homilist need not be perfect, just in love. As Pope Francis reminds the homilist: "We are not asked to be flawless, but to keep growing and wanting to grow as we advance along the path of the Gospel; our arms must never grow slack. What is essential is that the preacher be certain that God loves him, that Jesus Christ has saved him and that his love always has the last word. Encountering such beauty, he will often feel that his life does not glorify God as it should, and he will sincerely desire to respond more fully to so great a love."[6]

Many a homilist has confused a homily with other forms of instruction. This may be due in part to the influence of

---

[5] *Preaching the Mystery of Faith: The Sunday Homily,* Committee on Clergy, Consecrated Life, and Vocations, USCCB approved 2012.

[6] *Evangelii Gaudium,* 151.

Protestant ecclesial communion's concept of a sermon on the Catholic homily within the Mass. So, let's take a brief look at what a homily is not before we dig deeper into what a homily should be. Keep in mind that the homily may contain elements of what it, primarily, is not, but that these elements do not form the whole or primary body of the homily.

What the Homily is Not

The first home of the homily is the Mass itself. When we say home here, we mean that the homily *belongs* in and to the Mass. It is not a visitor or guest; it is not adjunct to the Mass, it is not the dictator or usurper of the Mass. The Mass is the first home of the homily; therefore, everything must be done and observed such that the homily is a beloved child within the home of the Mass; the homily is not an outsider, interloper, or stranger. Therefore, let's take a brief look at least a dozen things that homily is often confused with, that the homily is <u>not</u> meant to be:

The Homily is not a Sermon

A sermon is in many senses a free for all, a religious talk without boundaries. A sermon can be any length, any topic, and has few restrictions. A sermon is not part of the Mass, rather a sermon is the primary focus of the Protestant worship service. On the other hand, the homily is part of the

Mass and therefore occurs in a clearly defined liturgical context of specific readings, length, and purpose. The homily "is not a sermon on an abstract topic; in other words, the Mass is not the occasion for the preacher to address some issue completely unrelated to the liturgical celebration and its readings, or to do violence to the texts provided by the Church by twisting them to fit some preconceived idea."[7] Furthermore, the homily may not take over the Mass in length of time, content, or any other possible bizarre or inappropriate manner. It is part of the Mass; this cannot be forgotten. Unlike a sermon, it is not its own entity. Anyone can give a sermon; only ordained clergy can give a homily. This should make clear that it is part of the Mass, not adjunct to it. It should also make obvious that it is far more highly defined than a sermon.

The Homily is not a Lecture or an Adult Catechism Class.

While many things can be taught in homily and should be taught in homily, homily is not primarily adult instruction as one finds in a classroom. "Certainly, doctrine is not meant to be propounded in a homily in the way that it might unfold in a theology classroom or a lecture for an academic audience or even a catechism lesson. The homily is integral to the

---

[7] *Homiletic Directory*, Congregation for Divine Worship, USCCB (Washington DC, Libreria Editrice Vaticana, 2014), p.2.

liturgical act of the Eucharist, and the language and spirit of the homily should fit that context...Over time the homilist, while respecting the unique form and spirit of the Sunday homily, should communicate the full scope of this rich catechetical teaching to his congregation. During the course of the liturgical year, it is appropriate to offer the faithful, prudently and on the basis of the three-year Lectionary, 'thematic' homilies treating the great themes of the Christian faith."[8] Therefore, homily is not the moment to try to cram too much of the Catechism into parishioners. If your parishioners come to understand that God loves them, you love God, and you love them, then they will more likely come to your Adult Education Programs and other functions that you arrange outside of the Mass in parish life. Turning a homily into a mere information session is a disruption of its sacred function in the Mass.

The Homily is not a Partisan Political Pep Rally.

While political issues may certainly be addressed in homily, one must not forget that the homily has a specific function within the Mass as an act of love and the bridge between the Liturgy of the Word and that of the Eucharist. It is

---

[8] *Preaching the Mystery of Faith: The Sunday Homily,* Committee on Clergy, Consecrated Life, and Vocations, USCCB approved 2012.

not a time to take a stand on partisan political issues <u>not</u> clearly defined in Church teaching. But for those political matters on which Church teaching is crystal clear, still one must not allow the homily to turn into a political rally within the Mass. The subtlety of St. John Paul II's use of the word "solidarity" sufficed to get his political message understood without political badgering. Homily is not meant to alienate those of differing political parties but rather to bring them in line with Church teaching, grace, and the love of Jesus in the Eucharist. This in turn will lead to proper political, social, and moral actions. Highly recommended for your formation is *Forming Consciences for Faithful Citizenship - Part I - The U.S. Bishops' Reflection on Catholic Teaching and Political Life.* In it we are reminded that "The Church is involved in the political process but is not partisan. The Church cannot champion any candidate or party...The Church is principled but not ideological." [9]

There is much controversy concerning how, when, and to what extent to discuss political issues in homilies. Should the priest proclaim what is true especially in important election times? There have been, are, and will be times that political regimes threaten the very fabric of social moral life and persons are under direct and imminent threat due to their

---

[9] *Forming Consciences for Faithful Citizenship - Part I - The U.S. Bishops' Reflection on Catholic Teaching and Political Life,* USCCB, 2016.

ethnicity, vulnerability, societal status, and other ways in which persons are considered expendable from the womb to the tomb. Martyrs have died defending these persons and defending truth itself. Therefore, it is vital that Christians, and Catholics in particular, in reference to the homily, receive information regarding how to vote properly such that every individual vote upholds the moral law and an understanding of the priority level of the moral law. This priority clearly holds that right to life issues take precedence over state of life issues. There are many political/social issues that the Church recognizes can be tackled from many different points of view, but this is not true of all issues. The basic right to life at its beginning (the abortion issue) and the basic right to life at its ending (euthanasia) and any direct attacks on innocent human life in-between are not areas of political compromise. The faithful deserve a clear understanding of these basic truths.

However, the question remains as to how much of these truths belong in the homily. This goes to the root of the purpose of the homily within the Mass, which we will pursue later as information, formation, and inspiration—the Mass as a means to nurture, heal, direct, and unify. Therefore, it is generally recommended for priests with serious concerns about grave political issues to offer post or pre- Mass sessions rather than include the details in homilies. One can also point to copies of voter guides from the Bishops, which are generally available before major elections, to be picked up or handed out after Mass.

Lastly, there are differing political issues that fall outside the clear-cut guidelines of the Church in the details, such as how to deal with immigration. Taking a personal stand on these more nuanced issues within the homily serves only to divide rather than unify; again, outside of Mass one can certainly organize discussion groups for difficult political and social concerns.

When the Mass is the center point around which one's life revolves, the truths about political issues become clearer. Therefore, it is vital that the homily as a part of the Mass be suitable to the Mass and not become merely a political platform. One might consider the homiletic words of Father Paul Scalia, priest and son of the late US Supreme Court Justice Antonin Scalia, at his father's funeral Mass on February 20, 2016. Here, if ever, was an opportunity for political words during a homily. Fr. Scalia, after greeting the attendees, began his homily with this statement: "We are gathered here because of one man. A man known personally to many of us, known only by reputation to even more. A man loved by many, scorned by others. A man known for great controversy, and for great compassion. That man, of course, is Jesus of Nazareth."

Therefore, while a priest must always speak as his conscience, informed by the Church, dictates, he would do well to temper any essential political statements with the under-standing that we gather at Mass primarily for worship.

For the faithful, the "evangelization and the spread of God's word ought to inspire their activity in the world, as they work for the true common good in respecting and pro-moting the dignity of every person. Certainly, it is not the direct task of the Church to create a more just society, alt-hough she does have the right and duty to intervene on eth-ical and moral issues related to the good of individuals and peoples. It is primarily the task of the lay faithful, formed in the school of the Gospel, to be directly involved in political and social activity. For this reason, the Synod recommends that they receive a suitable formation in the principles of the Church's social teaching."[10] This formation may take place outside of the Mass.

The Homily is not a Moral Whipping Post.

Again, while morality must most certainly, at appropri-ate times, be addressed in homily, homily is not primarily a catechetics class on morality. The word of God "inevitably reveals the tragic possibility that human freedom can with-draw from this covenant dialogue with God for which we were created. The divine word also discloses the sin that

---

[10] *Verbum Domini,* 100.

lurks in the human heart…We are thus offered the merciful possibility of redemption and the start of a new life in Christ. For this reason it is important that the faithful be taught to acknowledge that the root of sin lies in the refusal to hear the word of the Lord, and to accept in Jesus, the Word of God, the forgiveness which opens us to salvation."[11] For this reason, one must be careful not to preach a Way of Life as mere moral behavior so much as a Person of Life Who leads us to appropriate loving behavior. We preach Christ Jesus. He in turn brings us to a way of life. Beating people up or tearing them down for their sins and failures is not the purpose of homily and often pushes them to further close their ears and hearts. "Be careful with your homily. Pity the people of God. Stop the homily abuse. Let your homily inspire and set hearts on fire."[12] The focus of homily is on the inspiration to virtue far more than the degradation of vice. "The need for repentance does not mean that homilies should simply berate the people for their failures. Such an approach is not usually effective, for concentrating on our sinfulness, unaccompanied by the assurance of grace, usually produces either resentment or discouragement. Preaching the Gospel entails challenge but also encouragement, consolation, support, and compassion. For this reason, many teachers of homiletics

---

[11] *Verbum Domini*, 56.

[12] Lingayen-Dagupan Archbishop Socrates Villegas at the Cathedral of Lingayen-Dagupan, April 2, 2015.

warn, quite legitimately, against 'moralizing' homilies, which harp excessively or exclusively on sin and its dangers. But when the offer of grace is also clear and presented with pastoral sensitivity, the recipient of that grace wants to change and wants to know what the new life in Christ looks like concretely."[13]

The Homily is not a State of the Union, State of the World Address.

The homily is not the morning or evening news, a broadcast for the fact that the culture appears to be rapidly falling apart. It is not meant to illuminate all the ills of society like a media outlet. We are well aware of all the shootings, murders, drug addictions, divorce rates, and families in crisis. "Nor is it fitting to talk about the latest news in order to awaken people's interest; we have television programs for that. It is possible, however, to start with some fact or story so that God's word can forcefully resound in its call to conversion, worship, commitment to fraternity and service, and so forth."[14] Those who come to Mass come for the solution, not to hear the obvious problems ragged about *ad nauseum*. You can certainly

---

[13] *Preaching the Mystery of Faith: The Sunday Homily,* Committee on Clergy, Consecrated Life, and Vocations, USCCB approved 2012.

[14] *Evangelii Gaudium,* 155.

address social and moral problems, but keep it short, simple, and liturgical. "The Church's urgent call for respect for human life, particularly for those who are most vulnerable, the call for justice for the poor and the migrant, the condemnation of oppression and violations of human and religious freedom, and the rejection of violence as an ordinary means of solving conflicts are some of the controversial issues that need to be part of the Church's catechesis and to find their way in an appropriate manner into the Church's liturgical preaching."[15] The "appropriate manner" is often sadly lacking in many a homily.

The Homily is not a Fund-Raising Event.

Homily is not the time to beg for money for the running of the parish. There is no reason this cannot be done immediately after the Mass is ended. The homily is not the time to discuss the leaking roof, the need for new carpeting in the sanctuary, or the outdated septic system. The homily is part of the Mass, not the grounds and maintenance committee or the parish finance committee address.

---

[15] *Preaching the Mystery of Faith: The Sunday Homily,* Committee on Clergy, Consecrated Life, and Vocations, USCCB approved 2012.

The Homily is not a theological dissertation.

The homily is not the time to show the parish how brilliantly cerebral is your wisdom of the exegesis of scripture, your eschatological comprehension, or your highbrow hermeneutics. It is wonderful that you have a grasp of anthropomorphism, immutability, coinherence, and the hypostatic union. Most don't. Can you ever use difficult terms? Yes, but clearly and immediately defined, few and far between. A covenant is a promise. Epistemologically speaking, there is no objective necessary condition that the homily be a portion of our ontological mortification. "In saying that the homily is none of these things, this does not mean that topical themes, biblical exegesis, doctrinal instruction, and personal witness have no place in preaching; indeed they can be effective as elements in a good homily."[16] Therefore, complex theological issues ought to be discussed at length, with clarity, and with the opportunity for questions in adult education classes where they are more properly placed.

The Homily is not a soliloquy or monologue.

This may come as a surprise to many, for one might say that surely the homily is not a dialogue. But the homily *is* a

---

[16] Homiletic Directory, Congregation for Divine Worship, USCCB, Libreria Editrice Vaticana, Washington DC, 2014, p.3.

dialogue! First of all, in homily the priest speaks *with* his people not *at* them. The priest should be seeking in his eye contact for their comprehension and assent in their returned eye contact, nod of the head, a leaning into his words; an interchange *is* sought in homily. This can only occur in dialogue. It might be helpful to think of the way in which a mother or father leans over the side of the crib and speaks to their baby. The baby does not speak back, but the mother or father's words are not intended as a monologue but the rudimentary elements of dialogue. "This setting, both maternal, and ecclesial, in which the dialogue between the Lord and his people takes place, should be encouraged by the closeness of the preacher, the warmth of his tone of voice, the unpretentiousness of his manner of speaking, the joy of his gestures. Even if the homily at times may be somewhat tedious, if this maternal and ecclesial spirit is present, it will always bear fruit, just as the tedious counsels of the mother bear fruit, in due time, in the hearts of her children."[17]

Furthermore, "the homily is intended to establish a 'dialogue' between the sacred biblical text and the Christian life of the hearer."[18] Additionally, "The homily has special importance due to its eucharistic context: it surpasses all forms

---

[17] *Evangelii Gaudium*, 140.

[18] *Preaching the Mystery of Faith: The Sunday Homily*, Committee on Clergy, Consecrated Life, and Vocations, USCCB approved 2012.

of catechesis as the supreme moment in the dialogue between God and his people which lead up to sacramental communion. The homily takes up once more the dialogue which the Lord has already established with his people. The preacher must know the heart of his community, in order to realize where its desire for God is alive and ardent, as well as where that dialogue, once loving, has been thwarted and is now barren."[19]

Therefore, one must never think of a homily as a one-way flow of words, but rather a meeting place of minds and hearts.

The Homily is not an entertainment performance.

"Now one comes to preach with mottos
and with laughs, and if he gets a good laugh
his cap inflates, and he's asked for nothing more."[20]

While the homily certainly ought not be tedious and boring, its goal is not to superficially distract. Priests in clown suits or floating on hover boards is best reserved for the parish supper in the church community hall. Often there is a

---

[19] *Evangelii Gaudium*, 137.

[20] Dante Alighieri, *The Paradiso*. Trans. by Daniel Fitzpatrick. *Dante Alighieri's Paradiso* (St. Louis: En Route Books and Media, 2021), Canto XXIX, Lines 115-17.

fine line between attracting and entertaining, but the line exists. Jesus attracted the multitudes without entertainment. The homily is part of the Mass and as such one must not lose sight of the concept of sacred time and space. It may well be a great feat in our cultural milieu of electronic and social media, computer games, comedy central, and entertainment tonight to keep an audience's diminished attention span, but the homily must be entrusted to the grace and work of the Holy Spirit, Who is anything but boring.

The Homily is not a history lesson.

While homily certainly begins in the past, it is not meant to get stuck there. While it is charming to know that Zacchaeus was short of stature and therefore up a tree when Jesus called him down, of far greater concern is that we too are spiritually short of stature, up the creek, and how can Jesus be of help to me today? Many a homily gets mired in the moment of 2000 years ago, rambling on and on about which person, who died 2000 years ago, did what when. "Whenever our awareness of its inspiration grows weak, we risk reading Scripture as an object of historical curiosity and not as the work of the Holy Spirit in which we can hear the Lord himself speak and recognize his presence in history."[21] Homily

---

[21] *Verbum Domini*, 19.

needs to bring it forward fast. Is history important? Absolutely! But it is not the primary point of homily. Unless there is historical information without which one cannot understand the lesson, move quickly from "they" back then to "we" here and now. This needs to happen before your homily is deemed irrelevant, which is usually within the first minute. This concept has also been referred to as the difference between exegesis and exposition; We can "distinguish between exegesis which asks: What did the text mean? and exposition, which asks: What does it mean today?...the word of God as it is attested in Scripture, and the concrete situation in which the congregation finds itself today."[22]

The Homily is not an echo.

How many times have we all heard the homily merely repeat the Gospel reading? We just heard it, and now we have to hear it again. Do you think that your audience is deaf? This monotonous repetition becomes downright painful when it is a long reading such as the Parable of the Prodigal Son. While repetition can surely be used for emphasis in the homily, to carry on as though we were absent for the entire reading is rather bizarre to say the least. Please assume

---

[22] Reginald H. Fuller, Daniel Westberg, *Preaching the Lectionary*, 3rd edition (Collegeville, MN, Liturgical Press, 2006), p. x.

that your parishioners got the gist of the story and talk *about* what it *means* for us today.

The Homily is not a Rant & Rag Session.

The homily is not a time for venting *ad nauseum* your disappointment with life, society's moral decline, church attendance, and/or the loss of the "good ole days". Everyone is struggling with deep and difficult cultural changes. Please don't waste precious homiletic time dragging us through your personal inconsolable mire of disappointment; rather refer to it, if you must, ever so briefly, and guide us, as well as yourself, beyond it, please.

The Homily is not a soapbox for dissent.

The faithful come to Mass to be fed in the safety and security of the fold of the Shepherd. They seek the security of Holy Mother Church. Hearing, via the homily, that their personal local shepherd, their priest, has a problem with Her is a breach of this refuge. We don't want to hear that you don't like the Holy Father, the Pope, for either your conservative or liberal reasons. We don't want to hear your dissent from official Church teaching, your beef with the local bishop, or your dissident feelings or inclinations on matters of doctrine, Tradition, and morality. It only serves to undermine the Mass. Waving dirty laundry from the pulpit, legitimate or otherwise, does not belong at the dinner table of the Lord. There may be appropriate times and places to raise concerns about the hierarchical runnings and leanings of the Church, but that time and place is never at the Mass. The Mass is never the time or place to raise your concerns or dissent about the latest apostolic letter, encyclical, or Church appointments. You have a captive audience, there by the command of Jesus, to receive the Word and the Eucharist for grace and holy unity. The homilist has no right to abuse this privilege with problematic issues that weaken the unity of the flock, subterfuge the proper goals of the Mass and/or undermine the ability of the faithful to go in peace.

It is important that homily be ever mindful that "the study of the word of God, both handed down and written, be constantly carried out in a profoundly ecclesial spirit, and that academic formation take due account of the pertinent interventions of the magisterium, which 'is not superior to the word of God but is rather its servant. It teaches only what has been handed on to it. At the divine command and with the help of the Holy Spirit, it listens to this devoutly, guards it reverently and expounds it faithfully'. Care must thus be taken that the instruction imparted acknowledge that 'sacred Tradition, sacred Scripture and the magisterium of the Church are so connected and associated that one of them cannot stand without the others'"[23] Never use the homily to go off the deep end.

The Homily is not a window for Theological Speculation

This includes your individual theological speculations or those of theologians within or outside the Church. "The homily is not an isolated example of biblical interpretation or a purely academic exercise. It is directed *from* faith, that of the Church and of the ordained minister who preaches in the name of Christ and his Church, *to* faith—that is, the faith of the Christian community gathered in a spirit of prayer and praise in the presence of the Risen Christ. Thus, the words of the homilist should be in harmony with the spirit and teaching of the Church. While the homily should be respectful of those who hear it and therefore be thoughtful, well-prepared, and coherent, the Sunday homily is not a time for theological speculation."[24]

---

[23] *Verbum Domini*, 47.

[24] *Preaching the Mystery of Faith: The Sunday Homily,* Committee on Clergy, Consecrated Life, and Vocations, USCCB approved 2012.

The Home of the Homily within the Intellect

The One Egg Homily

The young man had fallen on hard times and so he walked from his empty apartment to the local park and sat on a bench. He was hungry, really hungry perhaps for the first time in his life. He was deliberating on what to do when he looked across the park and saw the church steeple. He had never asked for a handout before, but he realized that if ever there was such a time, it was now. He pulled himself from the bench and walked toward the church. Once there, he knocked on the big front door of the rectory. Almost immediately the door opened, and a priest stuck his head out. "How can I help you, young man?" The young man briefly explained his plight and right away the priest said "Ah, no problem, I have plenty of food. I'll be right back." Momentarily, he returned and leaning out the door tossed the young man an egg which he caught in his right hand. Without warning he then tossed a second egg which the young man caught haphazardly in his left hand. Then without looking, the priest tossed a third egg which the young man tried to catch with both hands resulting in all three eggs smashing together and becoming a scrambled mess on the walkway at his feet. The priest, not noticing said, "You should be all set now, have a good day!" and closed the door. The young man walked away hungry.

The next day the young man went to another church. Another priest answered the door. Again, the young man explained his plight. "Hold tight," said the priest, "We have plenty of food; I'll get you something." Immediately, he returned and said, "I have an egg for you." "Okay!" said the young man nervously. "I am going to toss the egg to you, are you ready to catch it?" "Yes!" said the young man. "Okay, I will count to three and then carefully toss the egg." "Okay." said the young man again. "Catch with your right hand and cover it with you left, gently, since it is a raw egg, and you are hungry." "Okay," said the young man. The priest gently tossed the egg and the young man caught it. "Now be careful with that egg. Take it right home and cook it in boiling water for two minutes." "Okay!" said the young man. The priest nodded as he closed the door, but then stuck his head back out: "Careful now, it's not easy to carry an egg without breaking it, and just a touch of salt and pepper." "Thank you!" said the young man who then walked home carefully tending the egg until he could cook it and eat it. With just a touch of salt and pepper.

We are that young man as we hungrily enter the church each week to receive the homily egg. And if we get *the what, the why,* and *the how* of the message, we will be able to carry it into the home of the intellect and make good use of it in the home of the heart. Therefore, a homily should have only one theme; more than one theme and it all gets scrambled in our head. It needs to be clearly stressed throughout the homily so that we know what we are trying to catch. And then we need to be told why it is important for to us to hold it carefully. And once it is properly grasped, we need to be told clearly what we should do with it when we get it home to our everyday life. When these three things happen, the homily can feed us. When they don't, we go home homily-hungry. When the homily is effective, the homily moves from home to home, from the Mass to the intellect to the heart to the will.

The one-egg homily is of great importance because it is the link between our reception of the Word and our reception of the Eucharist. With the reception of this understanding of the word in place, we then move forward with a greater clarity to receive strength through the graces poured into us through the reception of the Eucharist.

The What, The Why, and The How of Homily

These are the three aspects of every good homily, however almost every homily we have ever heard leaves out at least the last one, *The How*, and often, sadly, the second one, *The Why*, as well. So, let's take a brief look at these three:

The What:

This is the easy one. *What* is the Old Testament reading, the Psalm, or the New Testament readings about? This is the

part the homilist plans to talk about based on his understanding of *What* the readings are about as God revealed to
him in prayer; *What* should be spoken about this day to these
people? The *What* you are speaking about needs to be clearly
communicated. The *What* is the shell of the One Egg. *What*
the eggshell is must be understood by everyone. *This* is what
the homilist is talking about today as we consider some aspect of the three or four readings, or just one of them, if there
is not a clear theme running through all of them. Many a
homily never gets past this stage, stuck in the *What*, because
it is *What* the homilist wants to talk about. It gets mired in
information rather than formation; the homily gets stuck
with the homilist.

The Why:

This digs a bit deeper into the purpose of homily; it is like
the egg white just inside the shell. *Why* is the *What* important? *Why* does this matter to anyone today? *Why* is
something from 2000 years ago of any consequence to us
now? *Why* is this matter relevant, applicable, pertinent to
our lives? *Why* should we care? *Why* should we listen to your
homily? *Why* will this make any difference in our lives, families, parish, community, world? The *Why* is the deep human
hunger (for the one egg) present in each and every one of us
in one form or another, but often in need of being revealed
by the homilist.

The How:

Now that I understand the What and the *Why*, *How* can I apply this to my life, my circumstances, my family, my parish, my community, my world? "So, a further purpose of the homily is to help God's people see how the Pascal Mystery shapes not only what we believe but it enables us to act in the light of the realities we believe."[25] This is the deep feeding nutrition of the egg. *How* can I do this in my life? *How* can I make such radical changes to follow this radical Love in my life? *How* can I make room for this in my busy life? *How* can I do this? This is where homily has the opportunity to point to the Eucharist because the answer to the question of *How* can I do it is the realization that I cannot do it alone. I must cooperate with Grace allowing Christ to work in me this transformation. Alone I can do nothing good. The *How* points to small steps toward actually embracing this holiness of which you speak. The *How* is the carrying and cooking of the whole egg. Without the *How*, the *What* and the *Why* get lost on the way home. The *How* is about formation of the will. This is why homily is not meant to be catechetical preaching which primarily informs the intellect. Granted that much has not been done on the level of catechetics for many adults in the Church, but this is no reason to mess up

---

[25] *Homiletic Directory*, Congregation for Divine Worship, USCCB (Washington DC, Libreria Editrice Vaticana, 2014), p. 11.

the Mass, but rather a strong reason not to confuse people further. When the Mass is strong, trust that all other aspects of parish life will flow from it.

Information-Formation-Inspiration

Information is the *What* and *Why* of homily.

You should be able to put this into one or two sentences; this is the one egg. It should be clear in your mind what you are hoping to convey and why. If you cannot clearly define what you are trying to say, what are the chances that anyone else will be able to decipher the message? Many a homilist will later say, "What I meant to say was…" Just say what you mean to say. Don't beat around the bush; get to the point and do so quickly. Information addresses the intellect for understanding. The information of homily is based on Holy Scripture and Holy Tradition of the Church as understood and taught by the Magisterium.

Formation is the *How* of homily.

Formation addresses the will. Formation gives life and form to concepts that are already basically accepted by the faithful. Formation works on concrete means by which the faith can be lived out. Formation is never abstract, but rather, always concrete. Formation does not just tell people to pray more but gives the concrete suggestions to pray while doing the dishes, filling the car with gas, waiting for the traffic light to turn green, while changing a baby's diaper. Formation gets down and dirty, into the trenches of real life. It cannot afford to be lofty, elite, or abstract. In other words, it must be connected to reality. It is not merely academic, speculative, theoretical, but rather concrete, practical, relevant. It is focused on specific persons in time and place seeking holiness in Christ Jesus. Homily must address the needs of this congregation, here and now. "Homilies are inspirational when they touch the deepest levels of the human heart and address the real questions of human experience. Pope Benedict XVI, in his encyclical *Spe Salvi*, spoke of people having 'little hopes' and the 'great hope.' 'Little hopes' are those ordinary experiences of joy and satisfaction we often experience: the love of family and friends, the anticipation of a vacation or a family celebration, the satisfaction of work well done, the blessing of good health, and so on. But underneath these smaller hopes must pulsate a deeper 'great hope' that ultimately gives meaning to all of our experience: the hope for life beyond death, the thirst for ultimate truth, goodness, beauty, and peace, the hope for communion with God himself."[26]

---

[26] *Preaching the Mystery of Faith: The Sunday Homily*, Committee on Clergy, Consecrated Life, and Vocations, USCCB approved 2012.

Inspiration is the personal *How* push to holiness

The pep rally, the confidence, faith, and hope-builder part of the homily. There is no point in giving information and formation if you do not give the strong message that to-gether, with the grace of God, we can get the job done! The homily addresses the hopes and fears of the people, these people, right here and now. It is not enough to say that we ought to go to confession (information), how we ought to prepare for confession (formation), but why we are so afraid to go, must also be discussed so that one can overcome our fears (inspiration). Therefore, the homily is familial in tone. It is not rhetorical elaboration, but personal encouragement to a mission of holiness. "Our encounter with Jesus inevita-bly leads to mission; our love for Jesus translates into our love for others. This is why the homily, which participates in the power of Christ's word, ought to inspire a sense of mis-sion for those who hear it, making them doers and proclaim-ers of that same word in the world. A homily that does not lead to mission is, therefore, incomplete."[27]

Many priests think that because people are so poorly cat-echized at this point in time, the priest therefore needs to turn every homily into a catechism class at the expense of the

---

[27] *Preaching the Mystery of Faith: The Sunday Homily,* Com-mittee on Clergy, Consecrated Life, and Vocations, USCCB ap-proved 2012.

homily. There are of course times when catechesis fits appropriately into the homily, as for example when Jesus preaches on the oneness of the Trinity and then one can easily integrate Church teaching into the homily. But this is not always the case! In fact, it is often just the opposite. If you can, in the homily, get people to understand that you love God, that God loves each and every one of us, and that you, our priest, love each and every one of us, then when you set up adult education classes outside of Mass, people will make more of an effort to come. If you build the house right, on rock, they will come to Mass and be strengthened to come back for more. If the homily gets waylaid by mere information or too much information, rather than the fullness of formation and inspiration to a mission of holiness that comes from the Holy Spirit, it comes undone. The homily must point always to the love and sacrifice of Jesus' for love of us. It is the deep love story of the Tri-Une God to His people, and the homily stands within that love story or else it fails to do its job as mission directed.

Chapter 2

The Language of Love

The Revealed and The Hidden

The revealed and the hidden refer to the understanding that the Mass is both a moment of Divine revelation and hidden Mystery, and as part of the Mass, the homily participates in both the revealed and the hidden. In the homily, within the context of the revelation of God's love for us, the problems, issues, and questions we face are now also revealed, while the fullness of the answers remain hidden in God and the future. Where will God lead me? How will I cooperate with God in the inner workings of my life and the mystery of my own human person? St. Paul tells us "For I do not do the good I want, but the evil I do not want is what I do."[1] The homily includes the *now* and the *not yet* for the Mystery of the Kingdom of God is *now* (revealed) and *not yet* (hidden). Therefore, the homily points us in the direction of learning to be patient with God, ourselves, and with those around us, encountering new depths of perseverance and discernment. So, too, the poet Rilke encourages us to "Be patient with all that is unsolved in your heart and try to love the questions

---

[1] RSVCE, Romans 7:19.

themselves, like locked rooms and like books that are now written in a very foreign tongue…Live the questions now. Perhaps you will then gradually, without noticing it, live along some distant day into the answer."[2] The homily requires that the homilist be aware of this twofold encounter with mystery and revelation, in both his parishioners and in his own life. Then one can begin to plumb the depths of *how* we are to dispose ourselves to receive answers to the questions.[3]

Beauty – Goodness – Truth

This is the order in which we learn best: beauty, then goodness, and finally truth. First a child sees the beauty of the world, perhaps a field of wheat dancing in the sunlight. Then he learns the goodness of this wheat, that it can be turned into bread and pancakes. Then he learns the truth of how much work and sacrifice will be necessary to accomplish this transformation, the sowing and reaping. Philosopher and author Peter Kreeft explains that if you see great athletic ability in a young girl and see the promise of her

---

[2] Rainer Maria Rilke, *Letters to a Young Poet* (New York: W.W. Norton & Company, 1993).

[3] Fr. Dominic Anaeto, Holy Apostles College & Seminary, personal conversation on *the hidden & the revealed in the Homily,* 2022.

becoming a ballerina, to pique her interest you would first take her to a ballet performance so that she might experience its pure lovely beauty. Eventually, this beauty would lead her to understand its goodness, and only then will she slowly be able to understand the truth of the personal sacrifice necessary to become a ballerina. The beautiful, the good, and the true are always an entwined trinity. This is the case with holiness as well; we usually begin our journey with beauty. And while there are many definitions of beauty, one aspect that is always essential is that of an abiding internal *order* as opposed to chaos.

"The relationship between the word of God and culture has found expression in many areas, especially in *the arts*. For this reason, the great tradition of East and West has always esteemed works of art inspired by sacred Scripture, as for example the figurative arts and architecture, literature and music. I think too of the ancient language expressed by *icons*, which from the Eastern tradition is gradually spreading throughout the world. With the Synod Fathers, the whole Church expresses her appreciation, esteem and admiration of those artists 'enamored of beauty' who have drawn inspiration from the sacred texts. They have contributed to the decoration of our churches, to the celebration of our faith, to the enrichment of our liturgy and many of them have helped to make somehow perceptible, in time and space, realities that are unseen and eternal."[4]

This is the importance of the beauty of the Sanctuary, the beauty of the Liturgy, the beauty of the Mass. And the beauty of the homily, as part of the Mass. When the homily becomes mundane, crass, argumentative, rude, impatient, unkind, unloving, impersonal, insensitive, flippant, abstract, confusing, or in any way disordered, it loses its beauty. Without beauty it becomes a "noisy gong or a clanging cymbal," an ugliness in the middle of the Mass. This is considered "abuse of the kindness of the people who are forced to listen to long, winding, repetitive, boring, unorganized, unprepared, mumbled homilies. In jest, but certainly with some truth, the people say our homilies are one of the obligatory scourges that they must go through every Sunday."[5]

Bring it forward Fast—History or His Story!

We have already discussed briefly the understanding that homily is not a history lesson, but let's take another moment to go into more detail what this really means and how it is accomplished. The Mass takes place in the now, the present moment of time. Christ is made present to us in the

---

[4] *Verbum Domini*, 112.

[5] Lingayen-Dagupan Archbishop Socrates Villegas at the Cathedral of Lingayen-Dagupan, April 2, 2015.

Eucharist. It is not symbolism, but a present living reality. The homily is part of the Mass; it too must be a present living reality. Therefore, the homilist must look for "clues for how to open a text in the new context of the community to which he preaches, where the ancient text is still alive and ever new in the moment of its proclamation."[6] This can be difficult at first for the homilist because the stories occurred in the past, the characters referred to lived and died in the past, the scriptures were written in the past. That's a lot of *past*-ness to overcome, but overcome it must be. For we, to whom the homily is directed, live our lives in the present. So, while it is beautiful to learn that in the past the wisemen brought gifts to the Baby Jesus, what then matters, in moving towards goodness and truth, is what do I bring Him today, in my present life? Do I bring Him gold, my best? Do I bring Him frankincense, my prayer? Do I bring Him myrrh, my death to sin? Do I follow the Star? If, as we claim, the Holy Scriptures are catholic, universal, meant for all peoples, in all times, in all places, then every scripture is meant for us today, now, in the present, and can be made so explicitly in the homily. Homily is rooted in the past, but always grows and blooms in the present.

"The relationship between Christ, the Word of the Father, and the Church cannot be fully understood in terms of

---

[6] *Homiletic Directory*, Congregation for Divine Worship, USCCB (Washington DC, Libreria Editrice Vaticana, 2014), p.9.

a mere past event; rather, it is a living relationship which each member of the faithful is personally called to enter into. We are speaking of the presence of God's word to us today: 'Lo, I am with you always, to the close of the age.'"[7] When homily stays encapsulated in the past, rather than merely rooted, it cannot grow, bloom, and bear fruit. It is a disservice to the Faithful to keep the Scriptures hidden under the dark basket of the past. Yes, it is harder work for the homilist to bring it into the light of the present day, but it must be done in order to thrive. And it must be done quickly. Often, a homily spends a long time rambling and meandering through the past and only in the last moment brings it forward, like a small fresh crumb that falls from a long stale loaf of bread. This is insufficient, to say the least. One primary reason is that by the second minute of the past-focused homily, most if not all parishioners, except perhaps the resident historian, have disengaged from a homily that does not in any way concern them or their life. It is mildly interesting to learn that Lot's wife looked back longingly on a life of sin and turned into a pillar of salt, but who really cares? Answer that question. Who really cares? Does the story of Lot's wife keep you up at night? No. It doesn't. What matters is that we do the same thing, every day, look back longingly at sin. And we don't know how to turn our gaze permanently to Jesus and

---

[7] *Verbum Domini*, 51.

move forward. That's what keeps us up at night, our anxiety, our worry, our lack of peace, the unholiness of myself, my marriage, my family, my work, my country, my culture.

There are many very simple ways to bring homily forward fast. Switching from past tense to present tense is one quick way to do this. Sometimes, Jesus does this for us, as in the cleansing of the ten lepers. "Ten were cleansed, were they not? Where are the other nine?" Notice that the first sentence is past tense, but the second sentence is present tense. A homily can continue at this point in the present tense. Yes, where are we, the other nine? Here we see a second means by which homily can be brought forward fast, switching from them/they to we/us. A third way of switching from the past to the present very quickly is to question at once who we are in the story account or in a parable. Are we the prodigal son of lust or the ungrateful son of pride? Are we Zacchaeus, short of stature, willing to climb even a tree to see Jesus? Or not? When Jesus calls, do we come quickly and receive Jesus with joy, bringing salvation into our homes? Or do we stay hiding in the tree, hoping salvation will find its way on its own to our home?

If your homily concentrates too long about leprosy and lepers in the time of Jesus or you get stuck discussing on and on about who Zacchaeus was, or the role of tax collectors at the time of Jesus, we realize very quickly that this homily is not relevant to my life today in this century. Leprosy and tax collecting are *not* the point. What _is_ the point of this Gospel for us today? Get to it! If your homily doesn't tell us, and tell us quickly, we stop listening and our attention drifts away. No one comes to Mass for an account of history. Rather, we wish to be incorporated into His Story in our lives today, now.

Preaching The Person of Christ Jesus as the Way

Homily often gets caught up in preaching a Way of Life rather than a Person of Life. It becomes a morality session focused in one way or another on the Ten Commandments. This was the Jewish Way of Life. Jesus comes to us as the fulfillment of the Law. When the disciples ask Him to show us the way to the Father, he clearly states that *He Himself* is "the Way, the Truth, and the Life."[8] Christianity preaches a Person as the Way. All other religions preach and point to a way of behaving, do this or do that. Only Christianity preaches a Person. Jesus says to the first disciples in the Gospel of Matthew, "Come follow me." Follow me. Me. This is a new covenant. You shall be my people, and I shall be your God. Get people to fall in love with Jesus and a deeper more personal reason for morality begins to follow; as St Augustine is often quoted as saying: "Love God and do as you please."[9] You will

---

[8] John 14:6 NRSVCE.
[9] Quote attributed to St. Augustine, referring to a sermon on 1 John 4:4-12.

never get people to stay in love with morality alone without a move toward holiness and eventually a relationship with Holiness Himself. You might get them to behave, but it may be a matter of fear of punishment rather than love of virtue. Love of virtue is a person integrated by grace in the body and soul. This does not mean that morality necessarily follows a turn toward Christ. Right views on difficult issues must still be taught, beginning with parents teaching their children. However, "The message of the Gospel is truly a matter of 'life and death' for us; there is nothing routine or trivial about it. If a homilist conveys merely some examples of proverbial wisdom or good manners, or only some insight gained from his personal experience, he may have spoken accurately and even helpfully, but he has not yet spoken the Gospel, which ultimately must focus on the person of Jesus and the dynamic power of his mission to the world."[10]

We are all on intimate terms with sin. We are not on intimate terms with holiness. This can only be done through a relationship with one, or all, of the Persons of the Trinity. We preach the Person of Jesus, the complete and perfect integration of beauty, goodness, and truth in the Incarnated Divine Person. Once your homily detours from that one primary understanding of the love of Christ Jesus for each of us,

---

[10] *Preaching the Mystery of Faith: The Sunday Homily,* Committee on Clergy, Consecrated Life, and Vocations, USCCB approved 2012.

Christ crucified, it goes off the rails. Again and again, the homily is part of the Mass. It all moves toward the Eucharist as the "source and summit of the Christian Faith."[11] The homily preaches the reality of Person. The depth of this cannot be understated. Philosopher Dietrich von Hildebrand once said, "Compared to the reality of a person, this chair doesn't even exist."[12] Another way to think of it is like this: You can fall in love with a place, a food, an academic interest, a form of entertainment, many, many, things in life, but nothing ever compares to falling in love with a person. A friendship, a marriage, a child, consumes your body, soul, attention, heart, like no thing ever could. Only the I-Thou brings deepest happiness, and yes, the possibility on human terms of deepest sorrow. The great poet John Donne cries out: *"Batter my heart, three-personed God;...take me to you, imprison me, for I except you enthral me, never shall be free, nor ever chaste, except you ravish me."* [13]This radical depth of love is why the homily cannot reduce Christianity to merely a way of life. Christianity is about the Love of Divine Persons.

---

[11] *Lumen Gentium*, Second Vatican Ecumenical Council, Dogmatic Constitution on the Church, 11.

[12] Stephen D. Schwarz, student and life-long friend of Dietrich von Hildebrand, heard this in classroom lecture.

[13] John Donne, *The Complete English Poems* (London: Penguin Books, 1983), p. 314.

This must always be implicit, and at times explicit, in every homily.

Heaven and Earth

Heaven and earth meet in the Mass in a multitude of ways. As we sing the Holy, Holy, Holy Lord, we are joined by all the host of heaven. The loftiness of the Mass can lead us to forget earth and slip into spiritual realms. But we are corporeal beings whose faith is not merely in the longed-for holiness of the soul, but the resurrection of the body. The Incarnation is made visible in a stable; it is messy business. It leads to the Crucifixion, sacrifice. The journey is difficult and dirty. There are feet to be washed. We search for the balance between prayer and service, Mary and Martha. I once knew of a woman who spent her days in prayer in her bedroom, while her five little children went hungry and unattended in the living room. This imbalance had dire consequences. To begin with, no one was fed. This imbalance can also occur within the homily in several different ways. When it does, the faithful are not fed.

Concrete vs Abstract Language: The loftiness of language can leave many who hear your homily having no idea what on earth you are talking about. The language of the seminary is not usually the language of the average person in the pew. "Preachers often use words learned during their studies and in specialized settings which are not part of the ordinary language of their hearers. These are words that are suitable in theology or catechesis, but whose meaning is incomprehensible to the majority of Christians. The greatest risk for a preacher is that he becomes so accustomed to his own language that he thinks that everyone else naturally understands and uses it."[14] This does not mean that big words can never be used in homily, but they must be explained. There is a difference between dumbing down the homily and making the homily concrete, meaningful, and understandable. It is easy to abstractly say that *we must love God* and *love others,* but what does this mean in concrete terms, in real life? Who are these others? I cannot feed the *world,* nor can I reach out to *humanity,* as the first is impossible and the latter an abstraction, but I can volunteer at the soup kitchen, and I might reach out to my brother who has not spoken to me for years.

Practical vs Impractical: The impracticability of your suggestions can often leave your parishioners feeling unable to move forward in their attempts at holiness. I once had a seminarian suggest that a mother of five young children, one of whom was a newborn infant nursing at intervals throughout the night, should get up at 4am before the children awoke in order to pray. A serious lack of a grasp of reality of the sleep deprivation in the household of a newborn baby. Suggestions to pray while changing diapers or while in the

---

[14] *Evangelii Gaudium,* 158.

shower were far more likely to be possible and practical as desperate times may call for desperate measures. Do your suggestions for moving into a life of prayer and holiness suit the actual lives of your parishioners? Very few people should be directed in the early stages of their transformation to the *Summa Theologica*, weeklong silent retreats, or hours of Adoration. One must think carefully of the actual lives of those to whom one directs in holiness. One must keep in mind as well the exhausted lives of those who work nine to five to keep food on the table and the rent or mortgage paid, especially those embracing the call to be fruitful and multiply. "Sad to say, in our days, and in the West, there is a widespread notion that God is extraneous to people's lives and problems, and that his very presence can be a threat to human autonomy. Yet the entire economy of salvation demonstrates that God speaks and acts in history for our good and our integral salvation. Thus, it is decisive, from the pastoral standpoint, to present the word of God in its capacity to enter into dialogue with the everyday problems which people face. Jesus himself says that he came that we might have life in abundance. Consequently, we need to make every effort to share the word of God as an openness to our problems, a response to our questions, a broadening of our values and the fulfilment of our aspirations."[15]

---

[15] *Verbum Domini*, 23.

Easy vs Difficult: Do you share with your parishioners the understanding that movement toward transformation is difficult? This is an honestly that is vital to the concept of the practical. The practical may be simple, but it is absolutely never easy. Grace abounds, but make no mistake about it, evil hates transformation in Christ. Virtues, the good habits of the soul, are not easily come by in our fallen state. Therefore, the practical must contain an honest assessment of the struggle involved. Otherwise, one may be left with the misconception that he or she is the only one who struggles, and this in turn leads to isolation, misery, and failure. On the other hand, knowing that we are all, including yourself, in the same difficult boat, offers solidarity, solace, and courage. Do not make light of matters that are difficult or painful to accomplish, rather acknowledge the reality of the challenges and complexities of doing the right thing.

Baby Steps vs Giant Leaps: Neil Armstrong, the first astronaut to step foot on the moon, understood the concept that if mankind is to make giant leaps, the individual man or woman begins with a small step. We are neither kangaroos nor superman. Attempts to leap tall buildings in a single bound leave us injured and broken. The fastest gold metaled Olympic runner begins his career around the age of one with his first baby step. And we are wise to do likewise in running the spiritual race of which St Paul writes, that we too might finish the course. Offering your parishioners the opportunity to start slowly, taking baby steps, and then to grow in strength and endurance, gives them the opportunity to get going in the first place. No one starts with a marathon or the 5000-meter running event. Make no mistake about it, training is an art. As a homilist and shepherd, you would do well to consider carefully the spiritual training schedule you recommend to your sheep, as well as your methods of encouragement and your willingness to run beside them in the race.

Order vs Disorder: One of the necessary ingredients for something to be beautiful is order. The Mass is meant to be beautiful and therefore the homily must follow suit. It ought not be disordered or chaotic. There are many ways in which a homily might be ordered, and we will explore some of these in greater detail later on. For now, suffice it to say that there must be inner order to the homily; it cannot jump all over the place with a random jumble of disconnected thoughts. It cannot jump back and forth in time. It cannot jump back and forth in concepts. It must have an organic procession that, simply put, makes sense. Many times, the homilist has simply too many ideas that he wishes to cram into this homily any which way he can! Scattered thoughts, ideas, concepts, thrown together with no thought to order. The mind loves order because we are made in the image of God who is Order. It takes time and energy to make sense out of disorder, a time and energy not allotted to us during the Mass. Just as one must put one's house in order, one must put one's homily in order. That is the work of the homilist and not the work of your listeners. This order must be clear, not vague or hidden. The homily is a beginner's map to holiness and therefore the highways and byways must be clearly delineated lest the faithful get lost.

Simple vs Complex: Your listeners get one opportunity to hear your homily, absorb its meaning, retain its content, carry it home, and then attempt to put it to work in their lives. One hearing only. You have spent time thinking about it, praying about it, writing it, practicing it; of course, you understand what it is all about! But we get one shot at it, one hearing. How simple is your message? Will it make it home? If your message is too complex, it will not make it out the doors of the church. We will shake your hand and say great homily with a dazed mind that hopes and prays that you do not ask us what we liked best about it. We might remember that it was well-delivered or that it left us feeling nice or perhaps it was funny. But we by no means take it home, incorporate it, make it our own map for the week ahead.

Whole vs Disjointed: There must be a thread that runs through the entire garment that can be clearly seen, understood, and when need be, used to draw and pull the entire thing tightly together. Is your homily whole? Is there unity? Is it a seamless garment or is it rather coming apart at the seams? Can you express your homily in one clear statement? Could you say to your listeners, hear, hear, *this* is what I want you to take home! Do *you* even know what you want *them* to remember? People hear and sometimes retain about 10% of what you say. Therefore, the other 90% must be the supporting structure for the 10%, not the other way around. What 10% of your homily is *most* important? (If you don't know, neither will anyone else.) How does the other 90% support the 10% such that there is internal integrity, unity, and wholeness?

Happiness vs Heaven: Highly theological concepts of heaven, eternal life, eternal rest, eternal beatitude, resting in the good, and perpetual light shining upon us are often difficult for many people to grasp in any concrete way that make practical sense to them. But if you speak of *happiness,* well, everyone understands some concept of happiness! The 4-year-old, 14-year-old, 34-year-old, and 94-year-old listening to your homily all understand happiness and desire it completely, regardless of what they think will bring them happiness. It is a universal concept. Therefore, it makes more sense to say that God desires you to be happy forever than that he desires you to live with Him forever. If you ask an unhappy person if they want to live forever, the answer might well be no, but if you ask an unhappy person if they want to be happy, the answer will be yes. Even if they do not believe happiness is possible. Presenting God's moral law as a means to happiness and sin as a means to great unhappiness can also be more understandable for many. So, find ways to focus more on God's desire for us to be happy, now, and forever, than on higher more abstract theological concepts of heaven and eternal life.

Overall, one needs to understand that "generic and abstract homilies which obscure the directness of God's word should be avoided, as well as useless digressions which risk drawing greater attention to the preacher than to the heart of the Gospel message. The faithful should be able to perceive clearly that the preacher has a compelling desire to present Christ, who must stand at the center of every homily."[16]

Homily as a Bridge in 3 Ways

As stated earlier, the homily has a specific role to do within the Mass: It is the bridge[17] between the Liturgy of the Word and the Liturgy of the Eucharist. "One of the most important teachings of Vatican II in regard to preaching is the insistence that the homily is an integral part of the Eucharist itself. As part of the entire liturgical act, the homily is meant to set hearts on fire with praise and thanksgiving. It is to be a feature of the intense and privileged encounter with Jesus Christ that takes place in the liturgy. One might even say that the homilist connects the two parts of the Eucharistic liturgy as he looks back at the Scripture readings and looks forward

---

[16] *Verbum Domini*, 59.

[17] I gratefully borrow this concept of "bridge" from Fr. Dominic Anaeto.

to the sacrificial meal."[18] We return to this concept here because it is of vital importance to understand that the homily does not stand alone; rather, it is grounded, like a bridge, in the two primary pillars of the Mass, while at the same time it unites them. Be ever mindful that "Scripture itself points us towards an appreciation of its own unbreakable bond with the Eucharist. 'It can never be forgotten that the divine word, read and proclaimed by the Church, has as its one purpose the sacrifice of the new covenant and the banquet of grace, that is, the Eucharist'. Word and Eucharist are so deeply bound together that we cannot understand one without the other."[19] "This is why virtually every homily preached during the liturgy should make some connection between the Scriptures just heard and the Eucharist about to be celebrated. Depending on what opportunities the texts in question provide, such a connection might be very brief or even only implicitly indicated, but at other times a firm connection should be established and drawn out."[20]

Is your homily grounded, to begin with, in the Liturgy of the Word? Many a homilist decides that the Word of this

---

[18] *Preaching the Mystery of Faith: The Sunday Homily,* Committee on Clergy, Consecrated Life, and Vocations, USCCB approved 2012.

[19] *Verbum Domini,* 55.

[20] *Preaching the Mystery of Faith: The Sunday Homily,* Committee on Clergy, Consecrated Life, and Vocations, USCCB approved 2012.

Mass is not of their choosing and go in search of different Mass readings. No, the Church in her wisdom has given you these readings for this day. To begin with, ground your homily in the solid rock of this Mass' Liturgy of the Word, not last week's or tomorrow's readings. Assume that as you meditate and pray over the readings that there is something in the Old Testament, Psalm, New Testament, or Gospel that the Holy Spirit wishes you to discuss with these people here at this Mass this day. This moment in time, for this particular homily, offers you a particular set of persons and circumstances never ever to be repeated.

Once the grounding of your homily in Holy Scripture has been accomplished and you journey across the bridge, your homily does not stand firm until the second grounding has been established, that of implicitly or explicitly pointing to the Eucharist as our primary means of grace. The homiletic journey is not whole without the two groundings. A journey across an ungrounded suspension bridge is not a homily, however interesting it might be in a different setting.

The homily is also a personal bridge between the priest (or deacon) and his people, the shepherd and his sheep. The homily is the moment in the Mass that makes this Mass stand out from all other Masses. It is a dialogue between this particular priest and these particular people, in this particular place, at this particular point in human history, never to be repeated. Even if used again, it is the stone thrown each time into a different pond. This is where the personal bridge is created in the parish. If it is done well, this bridge will be extended by other parish events that build up the parish life of faith. Does your homily show that you care about these people, understand their life circumstances and struggles? Does your homily share your own heart and faith journey? Or does it build a distinct wall between you and your people, as one Bishop was known to declare "We are all equal in the sight of God, from me all the way down to you!" Is your homily intimate or impersonal? Jesus tells us in John 10:14 that "I know my sheep and my sheep know me." Do you? Do they? This is the intimacy that the Gospels call us to in the Mass. "The homily is the touchstone for judging a pastor's closeness and ability to communicate to his people."[21] Furthermore, "TV has changed the way people expect good communication to be…They welcome the feeling that a friend is talking to them and confiding information, advise, cautions, humor, or some pithy information. TV has connected public speaking with intimacy."[22]

The homily is also a bridge between the Church and the domestic church, the intimate family community of life and love, the basic unit of every society. St. John Paul II reminds us in *Familiaris Consortio* (52) that the "future of evangeli-

---

[21] *Evangelii Gaudium*, 135.

[22] Alfred McBride,O.Praem., *How to Make Homilies Better, Briefer, Bolder*. Our Sunday Visitor, Inc. Huntington, IN. 2007, p.124.

zation depends in great part on the Church of the home." Therefore, it is vital that the homily makes it out the church doors, through the parking lot, and all the way home. This can only be done, and done well, if the homily is prepared with this goal in mind. The "one egg"[23] must be wrapped in such a way that it makes it home. The homily cannot end in the pew or in a congratulatory handshake at the door. It must make it home, supported by the grace of the Eucharist. Certainly, the laity bear a great deal of the responsibility in this matter! But your long, convoluted dissertation will not give them a snowball's chance in hell. To begin with, if you who wrote the homily cannot remember it, how will anyone else? Ask yourself just how much information you expect someone to remember (all the way home!) with *one* hearing of your homily?

I have often asked a seminarian or priest just exactly what he *meant* to say in the homily. The answer is often, "Well, what I *meant* to say was..." May I suggest that you just *actually* say what you *mean* to say?! During your homily preparation you might just ask yourself this vital question: What do I mean to say? Often, you will find yourself unsure, and rest assured that to the extent that you are unsure, so will your listeners be. What is the one egg that you mean to give, and what are your instructions that the egg might, by the

----

[23] See analogy at the beginning of this book: The One Egg Homily.

grace of God and the faith of the listener, arrive home, be cooked and eaten, thereby nourishing the domestic Church?

Preaching Forgiveness in Homily[24]

Let's take an important look at one of the most important themes in Holy Scripture, that of forgiveness. Everywhere in the Gospels Jesus speaks of the forgiveness of sins, and in the prayer he gives us, the Lord's Prayer, he calls us to forgive others as we have been forgiven. A lack of forgiveness is clearly a major stumbling block in both our relationships with others and our relationship with God, as well as the matter of self-forgiveness in many matters. The ability to forgive is a virtue, often not easily come by, especially in extremely difficult matters. Homilies are often prone to suggesting, alluding to, or demanding that we forgive others as though it is a commodity to be readily and easily picked up at the supermarket rather than a spiritual, and often painful, work of the soul.

Therefore, we include here a few basics concerning forgiveness that ought to be in the foundational understanding of those who preach on it. Granting forgiveness comes in two distinct forms: 1.) *Responding Forgiveness* which is when the offender is sorry and expresses this by saying "I'm sorry."

---

[24] Many of these concepts, as well as the forgiveness terms, are from Professor Stephen D. Schwarz, used with permission.

And 2.) *Initiating Forgiveness* which is when the offender does <u>not</u> say "I'm sorry." This may be because: The offender perhaps doesn't know they offended/hurt you, knows but could care less, knows but too fearful/embarrassed/shy to say so, or now far away from you in space/time or dead. In any case, you may never get an "*I am sorry*" from this offender. In these cases, the initiation of forgiveness must come from the one who was hurt rather than from the offender. Responding to a request for forgiveness is often easier than initiating, depending on the matter as well of course, but in either case it can be difficult and seemingly impossible for many people.

There are many confusions concerning forgiveness and what it entails. For example, in initiating forgiveness, you may or may not need to tell the offender of your forgiveness depending on the circumstances; nevertheless, you now hold forgiveness in your own heart rather than pain and anger. *"Unforgiveness is like taking poison and expecting the other person to die."* Forgiveness is a form of strength and power. Forgiveness does not mean you are a weak doormat; only a strong person can find the power to forgive. Unforgiveness, on the other hand, gives the power to the offender as you are the one who lives in pain while they may not.

When I have taught forgiveness in Ethics, students invariably ask about the really bad stuff in life such as murder, adultery, deep betrayals from friends, and almost always, the drunk driver who kills your child. How does one find forgiveness in one's heart for these persons? Like Corrie Ten Boom in *The Hiding Place*, can we stretch out our heart as she stretched out her hand to the ex-Nazi guard who tortured her sister? Only by grace. We start by the understanding that <u>we forgive the person, not the offence</u>. The offence just *was*; one cannot "undo" the past. Forgiveness is about the present and future. Forgiveness removes sin's power to continue hurting <u>*your*</u> soul. Forgiveness does mean "forgetting" in the sense that it is still in your memory bank, but it is no longer a barrier to common decency/friendship/relationship, if possible. *Forgiveness does not mean that you necessarily let the offender back in your life.* You may still need to protect yourself, but you have removed the anger and hatred from *your* heart towards the other *person*. (Or yourself in the case of self-forgiveness.)

Lastly, how is this forgiveness actually accomplished in the soul? Except for minor matters, most forgiveness is a *process* rather than an instant; forgiveness (especially granting, but sometimes also asking for it) can take months or even years to work out. But here is the crux of the matter: you are either working towards it or you are not; there is no middle ground. A recognition of how much God has forgiven us, and a gratitude for all we have undeservingly been given, is often a good starting place. Therefore, in homily, it is important to help others move in the direction of working towards forgiveness. Recognize that it is a difficult process, yes, but a strength that is accessible by grace, usually over time and through prayer. If the topic of forgiveness is overly simplified, it leaves listeners shaking their heads in disbelief and their hearts remain stone.

Urging the Sacrament of Reconciliation in Homily

Many are willing to come to the Sacrament of the Eucharist but far fewer are interested in coming to the Sacrament of Confession/Reconciliation. Therefore, it is a common theme in homily to urge parishioners to come to this other Sacrament of grace and forgiveness. So, let's take a look at the proper recommendation of this more difficult Sacrament. To begin with, it is not enough to just recommend something that most people avoid without looking seriously as to _why_ they avoid it. When my daughter Katie was very little, she had two toy boxes. At one point, we noticed that she played with all the toys in one box and never went near the other one at all. Finally, we looked into the matter and found out that there was a very realistic looking stuffed black bear in the second box of which she was terrified. Until the matter of the bear was dealt with, there was no going near that box of toys. The confessional box is no different for many; there is some kind of scary bear associated with it.

So, if you are going to advocate for this beautiful Sacrament you need to discuss openly the reasons people fear it. These reasons can range from deep embarrassment of sins to simple fears of forgetting the prayer of contrition. Many people think that they are the only one afraid or uncomfortable with this Sacrament and assume it is easier for others. Being open about the fears, _including your own_, that surround this Sacrament can be very helpful; open up the toy box and take a look at what's inside that evokes fear and keeps many from the joy of that other grace-filled box.

There are other misconceptions concerning this Sacrament that have arisen such as the true but inadequate concept that one can get forgiveness directly from God. Therefore, the sorrowful nature of sin, the understanding of forgiveness, the certainty of forgiveness, and the abundant reception of grace that comes from the Sacrament may need to be reintroduced gently to your parishioners. In any case, to urge your congregation toward a Sacrament that they either fail to understand and/or fear to enter in to, is futile. Rather engage your listeners with a deeper understanding of how we receive grace, and then deal directly with the fears associated with this very intimate Sacrament. Tackle the bear.

Chapter 3

First Things First

Homily Preparation

I am often asked in connection with my children's books the rather fascinating question: How long does it take to write a children's book? Seminarians often ask a similar question in regard to their homily preparation: How much time should it take me to write a homily? My answer to both questions is the same: A lifetime. For example, my children's book *Islands of Hope* required growing up in the Adirondacks without running water, traveling to India to see a far deeper poverty face-to-face, reading a book about Haiti,[1] becoming involved with building a village and digging a well in Haiti through Food For The Poor, the mission work of my parish, and many more life experiences. It required all of my being and experiences to write *that* book, at *that* time, for *that* audience. Fifteen years later, I am writing this book and not that one because this is the book God calls me to write today. In other words, every experience of your life will in some way shape your homily for this day, for these people of

---

[1] Tracy Kidder, *Mountains Beyond Mountains* (New York: Random House, 2003).

God. A stone will never get thrown into the same pool of water twice as the pool has been changed by the first stone. The question with every homily will be for you to ask what the Holy Spirit wants communicated to His people at this moment in time, through you. This is one of many reasons why downloading or borrowing someone else's homily is rarely a good idea. God wants to use all the experiences of *your* life, both good and bad, to speak in a unique manner and in a unique moment in time: at this Mass. Once you are more experienced, more fine-tuned, you will even find subtle changes in your homily from the Mass for the Saturday night crowd to the Sunday morning crew; they are a different part of the congregation. Also, even though the readings repeat every three years, your homily ought not. You, the congregation, and the times, have changed.

What is required of you for this to happen? What is required of God for this to happen? The awareness of the second question is far greater than the first…the understanding that God works on the homily with you. I once spent three months working on a manuscript about the massive earthquake in Haiti only to be told by my publisher that it was boring, uninspiring, and that I should try again with another story. But I had no other story. My well was empty. Embarrassed and dismayed, I fell into bed that night praying miserably for help, and as sleep came upon me, so too came the dream of the *other* story, the one God wanted known *through* me. In the following week I worked on the dream. That story, *Heal of the Hand*, got published almost immediately.

Prayer. Prayer. And more prayer. Lifting the heart and mind to God and listening for His response is vital to homily. It is very difficult for God to speak through you if you do not know Him. You cannot bring others to a life of prayer if your entire lifestyle is not one of prayer. Recommended is a life-long daily habit of *Lectio Divina*, the traditional practice of scripture reading, meditation, and prayer to find personal modes of communication between yourself and God. "Devote yourself to the *lectio* of the divine Scriptures; apply yourself to this with perseverance. Do your reading with the intent of believing in and pleasing God. If during the *lectio* you encounter a closed door, knock and it will be opened to you by that guardian of whom Jesus said, 'The gatekeeper will open it for him'. By applying yourself in this way to *Lectio Divina*, search diligently and with unshakable trust in God for the meaning of the divine Scriptures, which is hidden in great fullness within."[2] The homily is a mutual effort of work and grace, a living and vibrant creation flowing out of a personal relationship with the Triune God. "All the clergy must hold fast to the Sacred Scriptures through diligent sacred reading and careful study, especially the priests of Christ and others, such as deacons and catechists who are

---

[2] *Verbum Domini*, 86.

legitimately active in the ministry of the word. This is to be done so that none of them will become 'an empty preacher of the word of God outwardly, who is not a listener to it inwardly.'"[3] "It is that movement from prayerful attentiveness to the word to reflection on its meaning and to proclamation of the message in speech and action that undergirds the preaching ministry itself".[4]

"Long, winding, repetitious, irrelevant, unprepared homilies are signs of a sick spiritual life of the priest. Saint Joseph Cupertino said: 'A preacher is like a trumpet which produces no tone unless one blows into it. Before preaching, pray this way: Lord, you are the spirit, I am your trumpet. Without your breath I can give no sound.' It is not enough to prepare our homilies; the good priest must prepare himself. Preaching is a ministry of the soul and the heart not just of the vocal chords and brain cells. Our spiritual life is the true foundation of our homilies. The question is not what we will preach but rather who will we preach? We preach only Jesus Christ; always Jesus Christ."[5]

---

[3] *Dei Verbum*, 25.

[4] *Preaching the Mystery of Faith: The Sunday Homily*, Committee on Clergy, Consecrated Life, and Vocations, USCCB approved 2012.

[5] Lingayen-Dagupan Archbishop Socrates Villegas at the Cathedral of Lingayen-Dagupan, April 2, 2015.

Let us in our prayer not forget Mary, the Blessed Mother. "She speaks and thinks with the word of God; the word of God becomes her word, and her word issues from the word of God. Here we see how her thoughts are attuned to the thoughts of God, how her will is one with the will of God. Since Mary is completely imbued with the word of God, she is able to become the Mother of the Word Incarnate'. Furthermore, in looking to the Mother of God, we see how God's activity in the world always engages our freedom, because through faith the divine word transforms us. Our apostolic and pastoral work can never be effective unless we learn from Mary how to be shaped by the working of God within us: 'devout and loving attention to the figure of Mary as the model and archetype of the Church's faith is of capital importance for bringing about in our day a concrete paradigm shift in the Church's relation with the word, both in prayerful listening and in generous commitment to mission and proclamation'."[6]

First of all, know that your life speaks volumes before you ever speak a word. Secondly, since words ultimately come from your heart, your heart, whatever its state, becomes eventually evident to your parishioners. No one escapes the intrinsic connection of body and soul. Your inner state of soul eventually becomes your outer state both in body and in

---

[6] *Verbum Domini*, 28.

the words you speak. There is a wonderful story about Abraham Lincoln walking with a close friend when a third man walked by them. Lincoln turned to his friend and said, "I don't like that man's face." His friend replied that this was a rather uncharitable thing to say for a man cannot help what his face looks like. Lincoln replied, "On the contrary, by the time a man is forty years old, he is responsible for his face."[7] We would do well to contemplate the deep wisdom in these words. You are responsible for your face.

Grace. Grace. And Grace upon Grace. God gives as much as you are willing and capable of receiving. Pour yourself into the life of the Church, her sacramental means of grace, and a life of prayer. Seek and turn to Our Lady, the Holy Mother of God, through whom all grace comes. In thinking of grace, we might consider the analogy of the Upright Cup of philosopher Stephen D. Schwarz.[8] Imagine that grace is like rain pouring down in abundance. Now picture two cups, one is upright catching the precious rainwater, the second cup is lying on its side unable to catch a drop. Gratitude, an attitude of gratitude, is one of the most effective ways to turn your entire life into an Upright Cup capable of catching and retaining grace.

---

[7] Lucius E. Chittenden, Recollections of President Lincoln and His Administration, 1891.

[8] Stephen D. Schwarz, University of Rhode Island, Professor of Philosophy 1963-2007.

Virtue. Virtue. And more virtue. Fine tune the habits of your soul so that arrogance and foolishness may be replaced with humility that undergirds all habits of the soul and prudence that umbrellas the habits of the soul. Seek faith against despair, fortitude against weakness, justice against corruption, temperance against overindulgence. "Saint Jerome reminds us, preaching needs to be accompanied by the witness of a good life: 'Your actions should not contradict your words, lest when you preach in Church, someone may begin to think: 'So why don't you yourself act that way?' … In the priest of Christ, thought and word must be in agreement."[9] You would be wise to put on the full armor of God! Above all put on love. Love, as we know, willing the good of the other, covers a multitude of sins. And once more, I stress gratitude. Giving thanks to God in all circumstances. I often ask my ethics students: Can an ungrateful person be happy? The answer is no. And understand that gratitude is not only the individual act of giving thanks but an attitude that permeates one's entire life. It will also open your heart to the gift of homily.

Communication skills. Skills. And more skill. And yes, these can be learned. Here the willingness to practice, the humility to be corrected, and the desire to improve are directly connected to an openness to grace and the workings of the

---

[9] *Verbum Domini*, 60.

Holy Spirit. If you have a vocation to the priesthood, or the permanent diaconate, then you must trust that the Holy Spirit will supply, with your cooperation, that which is necessary to fulfill your vocation. With your cooperation. On occasion the art of homiletics may no doubt be merely given, but for most priests and deacons the art of homiletics will come with cooperation, honing, and hard work. Let us remember that where perfection is lacking, grace abounds.

Live the Word. God created the world in six days, and you have, in a sense, the same amount of time and eternity to create your homily. Yes, it includes all the previous time of your life experience and study, but now you must put it all together. This is an understanding of "the homily as a lifestyle"[10] where the word of God continuously penetrates every aspect of your life and being. Ruminating on the word of God throughout your daily movements should become the very homiletic lifestyle in which you live, and move, and have your being in Him. The homily is then no longer something that you do at Mass, but in fact, who you are. From this flows the homily that you share with others within the context of the Mass. "The ministry of the Word requires that the priest share in the *kenosis* of Christ, in his 'increasing and decreasing.' The fact that the priest does not speak about himself, but bears the message of another, certainly does not

---

[10] Fr. Dennis Kieton, *Our Lady of Victory*, Ashaway, RI, conversation 2021.

mean that he is not personally involved, but precisely the opposite: it is a giving-away-of-the-self in Christ that takes up the path of his Easter mystery and leads to a true finding-of-the-self and communion with him who is the Word of God in person."[11]

Do the Work. In practical terms, for the following Sunday Mass, begin on Monday with an in-depth reading and praying of the scriptures for the coming weekend. Then allow these scriptures to stew by grace in your mind and spirit. What stands out, and comes to your attention this day? "It is important to be attentive to the Lord's gestures on our journey. He speaks to us through events, through people, through encounters; it is necessary to be attentive to all of this. It is necessary to enter into real friendship with Jesus…to understand what he is asking of us."[12] Be attentive as well to the promptings and the silence of the Holy Spirit in your heart. Ruminate in silence, chew; ponder on it; this rumination is a form of prayer. Allow various ideas to roll through your mind and heart. Begin to shower, brush your teeth, drive, and sleep your homily; these are often wasted moments that need to be put to spiritual use. By Tuesday, you will have found the golden thread that will hold your

---

[11] Pope Benedict XVI, *Benedictus Day by Day with Pope Benedict XVI* (San Francisco: Ignatius Press, 2006), p. 322.

[12] Pope Benedict XVI, *Benedictus Day by Day with Pope Benedict XVI* (San Francisco: Ignatius Press, 2006), p. 329.

whole homily together, the one egg. By Wednesday and Thursday, you begin to add the ingredients of your life experience and theological studies to the mix. By Friday, you add the clear lines of formation and inspiration. By Saturday, you have the entire homily integrated into your prayer life, open to any finishing touches of grace that the Holy Spirit offers. (Obviously, generally shorter daily Mass homilies require you to refine this to the preparation process that works best for you.)

Remember that one is called always to "search out the intention of the sacred writers, attention should be given, among other things, to 'literary forms.' For truth is set forth and expressed differently in texts which are variously historical, prophetic, poetic, or of other forms of discourse. The interpreter must investigate what meaning the sacred writer intended to express and actually expressed in particular circumstances by using contemporary literary forms in accordance with the situation of his own time and culture. For the correct understanding of what the sacred author wanted to assert, due attention must be paid to the customary and characteristic styles of feeling, speaking and narrating which prevailed at the time of the sacred writer, and to the patterns men normally employed at that period in their everyday dealings with one another. But, since Holy Scripture must be read and interpreted in the sacred spirit in which it was written, no less serious attention must be given to the content and unity of the whole of Scripture if the meaning of the sacred texts is to be correctly worked out."[13]

The homilist should appreciate that the Church's teachings have developed in understanding through time and place in an organic manner and therefore he "should have the *habitus* of theology: the steady practice of reading the theological masters (both ancient and modern) and meditating on the great questions that they entertain. They should cultivate a real love for the writings of the doctors of the Church and study with eagerness the manner in which the Church's life and teaching have developed."[14] This includes a recognition of the many senses in which sacred literature can be understood: from the historical and literal to the spiritual, allegorical, moral, anagogical, eschatological, and perhaps other lenses of understanding. All of these, however, are intended to lead to "reading it as something present, not only in order to learn about what was once the case or what people once thought, but to learn what is true."[15]

------

[13] *Dei Verbum*, 12.

[14] *Preaching the Mystery of Faith: The Sunday Homily*, Committee on Clergy, Consecrated Life, and Vocations, USCCB approved 2012.

[15] Pope Benedict XVI, *Benedictus Day by Day with Pope Benedict XVI* (San Francisco: Ignatius Press, 2006), p. 328.

Homily Preparation Pattern

There is a basic pattern to the preparation of a good coherent homily:

1. Read, meditate, and pray the readings of the Mass of which you will preach.
2. Ask for the guidance of the Holy Spirit and the blessed Mother as to which line or idea is the most important for you to preach on in *this* homily. This will most likely change the next time these readings come along.
3. Find a solid concrete image (only one please) that fits with this idea from your life experience or another's, book readings, nature, the sphere of social or emotional life.
4. Work now to make every line of your homily revolve around this central idea and image that you have been given in prayer. This includes a clear understanding within yourself of how this idea is playing out in your own life. Weave the image you have selected throughout the homily so the idea gives coherence to the entire homily.
5. Explain it, show us how this is the case in all our lives today; move from past to present as quickly as possible.

6. Show us how we (you included) can gradually work to accomplish this aspect of holiness and/or relinquish this area of sinfulness in our own modern busy lives in the coming days.

7. Lastly, add encouragement by the very fact of our attendance at this Mass, our upcoming reception of the Eucharist, and inspire us by your love for us and Jesus' love for us to move forward in even greater faith.

Recently, my friend Deacon Costa Adamopoulos was working on a Gospel reading from Matthew. He settled in on the line "the people who sat in darkness have seen a great light."[16] Digging through his experiences of being in darkness, he chose a time of coming home at night and finding his house in utter darkness due to a power outage. Here in New England, where he was giving the homily, this was a common experience to which his congregation could easily relate, see clearly in their mind's eye. Then he took out his cell phone and turned on his cell phone flashlight and showed how this device had dispelled the "uncontrollable cold, perhaps even, fearful darkness" enough to "navigate the darkness." He went on to explain that Jesus is the Light of the world who can help us overcome the spiritual, emotional, societal, or familial darkness in which we all must navigate.

---

[16] Matthew 4:16 NRSVCE.

He explained that turning to the Light of Jesus can be harder to do than turning to use the flashlight, but just as necessary. He spoke of ways in which being generous to others, prayerful, and finding moments of silence to listen to God can help us turn on the Great Light with grace. He pointed to the Eucharist as a means for us to receive grace at this very Mass. We, here today, who often sit needlessly in darkness, can also see a Great Light.[17] Because these images of light and darkness were all coherent, relevant, simple, honest, memorable, and helpful, the homily had hope of making it home.

Beginning the Homily-the Take-Off

The first sentence of your homily is important. It begins the thread that you will weave throughout your homily. It is in the first 5-10 seconds of a homily that the listener decides if this is worth listening to or whether one should instead make one's grocery list for shopping after Mass. As already stated, please do not begin your homily with a joke or story unless it is integral to your homily. If your homily is good, it will not need superfluous entertainment openers. Your opening lines need to be strong, important, relevant, and believable. Don't reiterate the scripture reading. Don't get stuck in the past. Make it immediately clear why someone

---

[17] Deacon Costa Adamopoulos, Ashaway, RI.

should listen to you today. This comes with practice in integrating all the variables necessary for homily to go well. This practice period is where love covers a multitude of mistakes; if your congregation believes that you love God and love them, then they will allow you time to improve your homiletic skills. Time, not eternity. It is your responsibility to improve.

Look at your congregation and acknowledge their presence with proper eye contact. Don't think you can get away with looking at the back wall, side walls, or tops of heads. If you cannot even look at those to whom you speak, why would they listen to you? Persons acknowledge other persons primarily through eye contact. "I have watched homilists preach with downcast eyes, as though they are having a private conversation with themselves. I have seen others who firmly look at the back wall of the church. But people know when a speaker is ignoring them and today's congregations want the homilist to look at them."[18]

Choose your opening lines carefully. Think about what is most important in your homily and lead with it. Don't get bogged down with long descriptions, unnecessary details, ramblings; get to the point quickly. If you ramble or babble for 60 seconds or more, your listeners will be gone by the

---

[18] Alfred McBride, O.Praem., *How to Make Homilies Better, Briefer, Bolder.* (Huntington, IN: Our Sunday Visitor, Inc., 2007), p. 14.

time you get to the point. John commands our attention by his opening words *"In the beginning was the Word, and the Word was with God, and the Word was God."*[19] There you have it. A strong command of language is hard to drift mindlessly away from.

Whenever we have the occasion to fly in an airplane, we all sense how important the take-off and landing of the plane are to the voyage. These are the moments in which many of us pray, sweat, or wring our hands. So much depends on the proper take off and proper landing. You would do well to consider this image in relation to homily. Many a homilist gets all bungled up either on take-off or landing. Please do <u>not</u> begin your homily by saying *I am going to begin my homily with/by...*rather please just begin your homily! Imagine an actor coming out on stage and saying that he is now going to play Hamlet before he plays the part. Just *be* the homily.

It is highly recommended to practice and memorize your opening and closing lines, at least for a time. Taking off is the moment of decision for all involved in listening to you. Weakness, indecision, confusion, nervous prattle, foolish jokes, muddled concepts, and rambling story lines will all quickly lose your listeners. If we look, for example at William Shakespeare's famous soliloquy, spoken by *Hamlet*, we know well his dynamic opening line *"To be or not to be, that is the*

---

[19] John 1:1 NRSVCE.

question." There you have it. We know what the issue is. He commands our attention. And so must you in the opening line or lines of your homily. (More on landing later.)

To Ambo or not to Ambo

I do not want to address the more general controversy concerning from where it is most appropriate to deliver the homily. It is clear that in more recent years, certainly since Vatican II, many priests and deacons have chosen to leave the ambo or pulpit and deliver the homily in a less formal manner from the center area of the nave or while walking up and down the center aisle of the church. Given that this is the case, I want to address several issues related to this practice and make several suggestions before difficulties associated with this practice arise:

1. Keep in mind that the pulpit hides a multitude of problems. Your shaking hands have a place to grasp, your flailing arms are kept in check, your knocking knees are far less visible, and your cheat notes have a resting place.

2. Please do not leave the pulpit with plans to read your homily from sheets of paper or index cards in your hands. That is what the top surface of the pulpit is designed for, reading materials. So don't leave the pulpit if you still need your cheat sheets.

3. Generally when speaking, you should be able to see your audience and they should be able to see you. This gets messy when you start moving down the aisle while giving your homily. If you must, keep it very quick, as having your back to the front half of the congregation, who are now wondering if they ought to turn around to follow you, is not the best of ideas. I understand the temptation to engage in this charming connection with the people, but we have all also seen it become awkward at best and foolish at worst. The return trip to the front is never as elegant as the original dance down the aisle. So be careful in this regard.

4. The closer you get to your audience, the more tempted you become to engage them verbally in the homily. This can be good, or it can run amuck. Suddenly asking questions of particular parishioners, parleying with children, engaging in handshakes, and other interactions can happen spontaneously in these closer contact homilies. These can enhance the homily or can cause it to go off the rails entirely. Being aware of these possible issues is at least a starting point from which to decide how far from the pulpit you are safe to wander.

Chapter 4

Words Matter

Word Choice within Homily

Common-Use Words vs Infrequent-Use Words:

The more common use the language you use in homily the more easily heard and understood is your homily. Any words in your homily that are not readily used in everyday conversation ought to be rarely used, and if used, immediately explained. For example, don't use the word *covenant* if you can say *promise*, unless you begin with an explanation. "God makes a covenant, a promise, a sacred contract with His people." Pay attention to your use of vocabulary which, especially after theological studies, may be radically different from those to whom you preach. I recently heard an entire homily on the eschatological hope that we all ought to have. Excuse me? I doubt that more than five people listening had a clue as to what the homily was about.

Positive Words vs Negative Words:

Remember that often it's not *what* you say but *how* you said it. This refers to both your tone of voice and your choice

of words. I can tell you that you are fat, or I can suggest that
you might look better if you lost a few pounds. I can tell you
that abortion is murder, or I can tell you that choosing life
for the preborn child is a great good. I can tell you that adultery is a filthy evil, or I can tell you that the marriage bed is
sacred and needs protection from both spouses lest people
get deeply hurt. Negative words may be necessary in adult
education classes and theological lectures, but they are rarely
of good use in a homily. The homily is part of the Mass, the
table of the Lord. What do you deem appropriate to say at
your own dinner table? Remember that the faithful *must* attend Mass; it is not optional; they are in a sense a captive audience who cannot escape your words, be those words compassionate or harsh. If you are harsh from the pulpit, do not
be surprised if no one dares approach you with their sins in
the confessional. There is a difference between compassionate directness of moral direction and severely harsh admon-
ition. Work hard to learn where the line is and stay well clear
of it. Remember that words matter and that positive words
attract attention to what is being preached; they attract like
honey rather than the vinegar of negative words. A good
homily "is not so much concerned with pointing out what
shouldn't be done, but with suggesting what we can do better. In any case, if it does draw attention to something negative, it will also attempt to point to a positive and attractive
value, lest it remain mired in complaints, laments, criticisms
and reproaches. Positive preaching always offers hope,

points to the future, does not leave us trapped in negativity."[1] Think of how Confession has become Reconciliation, because the latter focuses of the *positive out-come* while the former focused on the *in-going difficulty* of confessing one's sins. "Some people think they can be good preachers because they know what ought to be said, but they pay no attention to how *it* should be said... They complain when people do not listen to or appreciate them, but perhaps they have never taken the trouble to find the proper way of presenting their message."[2] To be as gentle as the dove and as sly as the fox comes well recommended.

Communal Words vs. Separating Words:

Always include yourself in your homily! Unless you are talking about your own personal story in your homily, take the unholy trinity of *Me, Myself, & I* out of it, as well as the exclusive term of *You*. Almost everywhere a pronoun is necessary in the homily it would be best use *We* or *Us* or *You & I*. So rather than a message in which you are not included, in which you separate yourself from your listeners, you acknowledge that you are in the boat with them, all together in need of the Lord. So, *we* acknowledge that we are all called by Jesus. *You and I* need the grace offered by going to

---

[1] *Evangelii Gaudium*, 159.
[2] *Evangelii Gaudium*, 156.

Reconciliation, which can be difficult for *all of us*. The Church invites *us* to find moments of prayer each day. This language of inclusivity removes any semblance of superiority or arrogance on the part of the homilist. Make sure that there is no "from me all the way down to you" insinuated into your homily.

What has been said of poetry can just as rightly be said of the homily: "Make sure there is nothing in the poem that would keep the reader from becoming the speaker of the poem...The poem in which the reader does not feel himself or herself a participant is a lecture, listened to from an uncomfortable chair, in a stuffy room, inside a building."[3]

Therefore, understand that "the preacher needs to speak in such a way that his hearers can sense his belief in the power of God. He must not lower the standards of his message to the level of his own personal witness, fearing that he will be accused of not practicing what he preaches. Since he is preaching not himself but Christ, he can, without hypocrisy, point out the heights of sanctity, to which, like every other individual, in his pilgrim faith he is aspiring."[4]

---

[3] Mary Oliver, *Winter Hours* (New York: Mariner Books, 1999), p. 25.

[4] *Homiletic Directory*, Congregation for Divine Worship, USCCB (Washington, DC: Libreria Editrice Vaticana, 2014), p. 3.

Hygienic Words vs Unhygienic Words:

Words can be unseemly and/or problematic in a number of ways:

First of all, there is the obvious use of language as decent or vulgar, clean or dirty. Suffice it to say that swear words ought never to be used in homily, including more common vulgar expressions that have drifted into ordinary use such as "pissed off." While one might think that the use of such words helps to make you look cool, casual, or comfortable, it may only serve to make you look crass.

Beware as well of social expressions that have mixed or double meanings, sexual inuendo, or new usages. For example, thirty years ago *to hook up* meant to meet for coffee, while now it means to meet for sex. To the 90-year-old in the pew the word *gay* means *happy*, to the 40-year-old it means *homosexual* and now, to the teenager it can mean *homosexual* or *stupid.*, depending on the context. Terms like *Daddy* and *Happy Ending* now have extremely sexual colloquial/slang meanings to the young adults in your congregation. Be in the world but not of it and stay tuned as best possible to changes in the cultural language. If you see snickering or giggling during your homily, make it your priority to find out why.

Secondly, there are words that are intrinsically connected to sexuality in ways that are merely mentally disruptive to the listener. Recently, I heard a wonderful deacon mention in a homily that the Gospel of John is *pregnant with meaning*. While Mary can be pregnant with the Baby Jesus, it is best that the Gospel of John not be in the family way. It suffices to say that the Gospel of John is *full of meaning, overflowing* if you are particularly exuberant. This is not because *pregnant* is a dirty word, but because it is, well, pregnant with meaning, some of which is distracting and leads one down a path you do not intend your listener to go. There are many words that have connotative meanings that go far beyond their denotative meaning. Be on the lookout for them.

Thirdly, there are words that are jarring when that is not your intent. *Abortion, Adultery, Miscarriage, Divorce, and Pornography,* to name a few, are words that are loaded with pain and hurt for many people. This does not mean that you can never use them, but that they must be used with extreme pastoral care, especially if used in the homily. Remember that the faithful come to the Mass for conversion and grace not aversion and disgrace; therefore, this mercy and compassion must ever be in the mind of the shepherd. Lastly, please save discussions of *sexual frustration* and *masturbation* for some appropriate (uni-sex) teaching event other than the homily.

Fourth, it is understood that Holy Scripture refers to Satan (the devil) and the evil fallen angels and that we call upon

St. Michael the Archangel to "defend us in the battle"[5] against these powers of darkness that war against both the people of God and the Kingdom of God. Many Catholics informed by Church teaching and proper catechesis understand that the "power of Satan is, nonetheless, not infinite. He is only a creature, powerful from the fact that he is pure spirit, but still a creature."[6] However, upon hearing the words *exorcism* or *exorcist* those parishioners, who have been catechized regarding evil spirits primarily by the media and scary films, will be completely distracted from the rest of the content of your homily. These realities require careful explanation and in-depth clarifications that usually cannot be accomplished in the context and time frame of the homily. Therefore, in the homily, be aware of language alternatives, such as *casting out of evil spirits,* that will not lead to unnecessary sensational imagery.

Fifth, "whether commenting on other faith communities or on the secular culture in which we are immersed, the homily is not a place for bitter invective, coarse rhetoric, or stereotypes and caricatures of other people's religious tradi-

---

[5] Prayer to St. Michael the Archangel, Pope Leo XIII, 1886.
[6] *Catechism of the Catholic Church*, 395.

tions or ethnic backgrounds."[7] Be aware that these can sneak in inappropriately, especially under the guise of humor.

Sixth, there should be no derogatory name-calling of any persons. A homily given recently referred to an actual person, although unnamed, as "stupid" due to a decision and action of which the priest disapproved and which was described in detail in the homily. It was obvious that parishioners could possibly figure out who the "stupid" offender was and therefore this amounted to a public verbal flogging. This is improper in homily, as it would be deplorable in any loving conversation. To begin with, actual private individual's sins, mistakes, and foolish decisions are best not discussed in the homily in any identifiable manner. And it's best to remember that while we can judge actions, we cannot judge persons, so while one might call an action foolish, insulting name-calling of persons is unacceptable.

Lastly, especially important is the appropriate use of language and topic during the family or children's Mass. I once heard a homilist discussing in great detail a recent local rampage of murder at an elementary school when he suddenly realized that he was speaking at the monthly family Mass. The priest was mortified, the congregation was horrified, and the situation was not reparable. So be mindful that

---

[7] *Preaching the Mystery of Faith: The Sunday Homily,* Committee on Clergy, Consecrated Life, and Vocations, USCCB approved 2012.

murder, divorce, pornography, fornication, and abortion are usually best not discussed at the children's Mass. Children are often present at all Masses and this needs to generally be kept in mind, but a children's Mass is designed with them primarily in mind and ought to be tailored to their sensibilities.

Be aware also that the Scandal has changed everything. I once heard a well-meaning deacon-in-training mention in a practice homily that little Suzy gave him a crayon drawing of her bedroom. No. No. No. No mention of children and bedrooms, bathrooms, or any other private spaces ought ever to be mentioned in the same paragraph. If, for example, you want to encourage children to pray when they go to bed, use terms like "at bedtime or before you go to sleep at night." Innocent times are over. It is sad, but it is a reality. Be very careful in homily of what you say about children in general and of any child in particular.

Invitational words vs Demanding Words:

It is important to issue invitations rather than demands. In short, no one likes to be told what to do. As children are quick to point out to older siblings: You ain't the boss of me! There is a massive psychological difference between telling someone that they "must or ought to fast during Lent" and in rather saying that during the season of Lent the Church "invites each and every one of us to fast." God never breaches our free will and neither should your homily. The homily instructs not by telling parishioners how they ought to lead their lives, but by inviting them into the life of the Church and her Lord.

Be on the lookout for phrases in your homily like *You ought to...you ought not...you need to do...you should...you better do...you have to...don't forget to...* These sentiments are often met with an attitude of resentment and resistance. Rather use phrases such as "The Church invites us to..., we are called to participate in...,wouldn't it be wonderful if we could all try to...,would it perhaps help our lives if we...,we are encouraged at this time to..., I ask you if during this time we could together...,may we consider supporting one another during this Advent to remember to come together in prayer..."

There are many ways to ask, encourage, invite, request, enjoin, inspire, call, and/or recommend the opening of the soul to new life in Christ rather than by demand. Invitations are such a positive manner of being called upon that we have made them into an expensive enterprise from birthdays to weddings to anniversary gatherings. To be invited is to be loved! Use the concept of invitation liberally in your homily. Invitation also by its very nature tends to lean toward inclusive language. I demand of you becomes we are invited. The demand to climb the arduous mountain becomes an invitation to journey together to heights unimagined.

Promises vs Qualified Promises

It is very easy to slip into making promises for God within the homily without clearly qualifying what that promise actually means. For example, simply saying that "*God always answers our prayers*" can be a minefield without the necessary qualification. Yes, He does, but sometimes the answer is No, or Not Now. Imagine the young parents sitting there listening to your homily; they prayed for three years, day and night, that their sick little child wouldn't die, but she did die. Their prayers and faith didn't save her from death in this life. Did God not hear their prayers? Of course, He did! But for some greater good that we certainly cannot imagine, His permissive will allowed her death. They may well not <u>feel that</u> God answered their prayers at all. Your unqualified statement may leave them questioning their faith altogether or blaming one another for a lack of faith. Other such promises, taken out of the greater context of understanding, can also become a quagmire in homily: *Good always wins in the end. Everyone who comes to Jesus will be healed. Prayer will always bring you comfort. Ask and you will receive. Seek and you will find. Knock and the door will be opened.* These promises from God are not free-for-alls. They exist within a context of precise meaning which can easily be misconstrued, especially by those in emotional or spiritual pain. Be careful with promises.

Use of Story in Homily

As we all know, Jesus used stories and parables in his teachings to the apostles and the crowds. I have long been a part of the storytelling community in Rhode Island both as a listener and as a coach for tellers. Everyone loves a good story. In the storytelling community, the saying is that there is nothing better than a good story, but it goes on to state that there is nothing worse than a bad story. Often, a bad story takes the form of being two to three times longer than necessary, so get to the point and weed out extraneous details. And for God's sake, know your story! It's a story, not a theological dissertation. Why are you reading it? You wouldn't read it at a party; you would just tell it. If you have to read it, it hasn't become your story to tell.

"The special power of the parable is to engage the listener about its meaning. Artful human speech, especially in stories, can appear to veil truth for those who do not engage it and yet can reveal truth for those willing to listen and ponder its meaning. Some cultures in particular relish stories that bring home to them the practical wisdom of the Gospel. Jesus did not simply lecture his audiences but enticed them by evoking experiences they were invited to think about and try to understand. Being an effective storyteller may not be a gift that comes easily to everyone who must preach, but the lesson here is that the homilist must have empathy for human experience, observe it closely and sympathetically, and incorporate it into his preaching."[8]

A good story has two components; its content is good and how it is told is good. If either of these is off the rails, then the story experience fails as story. The connection between the two is often the teller's familiarity with the story and the teller's personal interest in the story. Never tell a story that you don't love is the rule of thumb to begin with. Even a sad story must be loved for some intrinsic reason such as what can be learned from it. Stories are not meant to merely entertain or to take up space in your homily, but rather are intended to convey meaning and add depth to a homily. So please don't tell a story that does neither.

Stories tend to fall into two primary categories: pretend stories (fiction) and actual life stories (non-fiction). Goldilocks and the Three Bears is the former, while a story about the time you actually got lost in the woods is the latter. Both should contain revealing truths about reality in order to be good stories. However, just because you have a good story, does not mean that it belongs in this homily. The story must be organic to the ideas of the Liturgy of the Word. In other words, it must make sense to all present as to why you are

---

[8] *Preaching the Mystery of Faith: The Sunday Homily,* Committee on Clergy, Consecrated Life, and Vocations, USCCB approved 2012.

telling this story within this particular Mass. If there is any doubt, make the connection crystal clear or leave it out.

Many a homilist is tempted to tell a funny story to entertain or get the congregation jovial; don't. The homily is part of the Mass, not comedy central. That being said, a funny story can certainly be used to show a deeper point of the readings. It is not that humor is not allowed, but that if humor is used, it must always be in service of a higher good within the Mass. Humor that is used for lesser goods such as making Father look like the local cool comedian should be reserved for the parish supper entertainment. Furthermore, "it is equally important to caution those who have no native sense of humor from trying to be funny…To a person without humor-whatever the mysterious reason for this-the world may look witty, and he can get a laugh out of it, but he lacks the funny bone to translate it into an amusing remark. In this case, he wisely uses other rhetorical gifts to create a persuasive homily…Also because humor is equated with entertainment in our culture, it's prudent to use it sparingly in homilies."[9]

Life stories that you would like to share with your congregation must be considered with even more care. Many of us have learned vital lessons from our life experiences and

---

[9] Alfred McBride, O.Praem., *How to Make Homilies Better, Briefer, Bolder.* (Huntington, IN: Our Sunday Visitor, Inc., 2007), p. 76-77.

we would like to share those experiences and subsequent lessons learned with others. Here the priest or deacon must tread carefully and respectfully within his vocation. The congregation should never hear about the time you did drugs, got caught drunk driving, or any other such confusing behaviors. Nor should they hear about your sister's abortion or that your father was abusive to your mother. In other words, your dirty laundry does not get aired, ever, in homily. No matter what you may personally have learned from it. No one wants to leave Mass wondering what else you've done or just how dysfunctional your upbringing really was. If there is a lesson from your rough past that you feel called to share, you might begin with the notion that "I once knew a man who..." That the man you "once knew" was yourself is not necessary to the listeners of the story nor should they be privy to this connected information.

Remember that the homily is not about you. Your shared life story must have a deeper meaning that connects us with each other and God without waving any red flags about your character. "The goal of the homily is to lead the hearer to the deep inner connection between God's word and the actual circumstances of one's everyday life. In some instances one's own experience—told in an appropriate way without drawing too much attention to oneself—can also be effective, especially when this experience is one that resonates with similar experiences of those with whom it is shared."[10]

In the Catholic Church, for late vocation priests who were previously married and later widowed or annulled, permanent deacons who are married, and married clergy from other denominations that have crossed the Tiber, let's briefly discuss the mentioning of the wife, kids, or grandkids in the homily. First of all, while many of your parishioners know you, there may always be visitors who don't. In the Roman Church, we currently have the discipline of a *primarily* unmarried clergy. Keep that in mind, lest confusion occur. If the wife, ex-wife, kids, or grandkids are mentioned in your homily, make sure your status in the church regarding them is clear. Whenever possible leave them out; the muddled misunderstandings are endless. I once, while on vacation, thought I had gone to an Anglican Church by mistake when the priest discussed his children in the homily. (Needless to say, this is not an issue in other ecclesial communities, but must be recognized as a concern for homily within the Latin Rite.)

Personal stories that correspond to the Liturgy of the Word in some meaningful way are certainly to be considered for the homily. People usually find real life stories enjoyable,

---

[10] *Preaching the Mystery of Faith: The Sunday Homily,* Committee on Clergy, Consecrated Life, and Vocations, USCCB approved 2012.

understandable, relatable, and most importantly, memorable. When a story is clearly connected to a life lesson, it can be of great value. It is also a means of sharing your life with your parishioners. But keep in mind that your life must be one of continued study and striving for holiness! Otherwise, the "homily becomes our story and not the story of Jesus."[11]

In most parishes about 10% of parishioners take a more active role in parish life than the rest of the flock, ranging from religious education teaching, youth ministry, music ministry, church decorating, parish dinners and bazaars, to membership on the parish council, to building and grounds committees, and/or to daily Mass participation. This proactive connection within the parish allows the clergy to get to know this 10% of the laity, and vice versa. But for the vast majority, Sunday Mass is their only opportunity to get to know you, and this can primarily be accomplished only in the homily. When you share your life stories within the homily, you reach out not merely liturgically but personally, and this can encourage a more proactive response from those who might otherwise remain aloof.

---

[11] Lingayen-Dagupan Archbishop Socrates Villegas at the Cathedral of Lingayen-Dagupan, April 2, 2015.

Seal of Confession & Homily

Lastly, but of great importance, let us briefly mention stories that are heard under the Seal of Confession. You would be surprised to know how often these stories can inadvertently slip into a homily. So be here cautiously reminded of the Code of Canon Law: "The sacramental seal is inviolable; therefore it is absolutely forbidden for a confessor to betray in <u>any way</u> a penitent in words or in any manner and for any reason (983). A confessor is prohibited completely from using knowledge acquired from confession to the detriment of the penitent even when any danger of revelation is excluded (984)."[12] Hence, common sense says that it is usually best not to provide any information that could unintentionally reveal a person's sins. *This usually includes even revealing merely that a person <u>has been</u> to confession if this could potentially lead to the revelation of the sin itself.* There is the old joke about Fr. John who tells at his retirement party of his very first penitent, that the man confessed to murdering his wife; then an elderly gentleman comes in late to the party and announces, to the horror of all present, that he was Fr. John's very first penitent. Oops. Be extremely careful what you share in a homily, especially avoiding anything spoken under the sacred seal of confession.

---

[12] *Code of Canon Law*, 2021.

The Use of the Metaphor in Homily

Jesus certainly understood the use of metaphor (and analogy and simile) in speaking to the Apostles and the crowds. He is the Bread of Life. He is the Good Shepherd. He is the Living Water. "One of the most important things is to learn how to use images in preaching, how to appeal to imagery. Sometimes examples are used to clarify a certain point, but these examples usually appeal only to the mind; images, on the other hand, help people better to appreciate and accept the message we wish to communicate. An attractive image makes the message seem familiar, close to home, practical and related to everyday life. A successful image can make people savor the message, awaken a desire and move the will towards the Gospel."[13] Metaphor will often be the ribbon that runs through your homily, the central theme that holds it all together. It is therefore important that you stick to one idea and do not mix metaphors which lead to incongruous concepts and confusion. For example: *Jesus is the good Shepherd who wants to bring you home to the hive. When you go to confession you clean your car and in so doing hit a home run. The darkness of sin is like being locked in a dark room and being unable to get out of the mud. Spiritual growth brings you into the light and gets you out of the sinking*

---

[13] *Evangelii Gaudium*, 157.

boat. It is all too common in working on a homily to start with one idea and along the way another similar concept pops into your head and you switch gears without even realizing, jump the track, go down a rabbit hole, and sink the whole ship. See?!

The Devil is in the Details

Best therefore to generally avoid the details! Many a homily gets lost in details that are unnecessary and outside the general point of the homily; these are time wasting nuggets that might be of interest were this primarily an educational lecture, but it is not. Many a homilist wants to discuss the details of sycamore trees, figs, vineyards, money used in ancient times, habits of sheep, earthenware jars, the molecular structure of yeast in bread-making, and the entire landscape, architecture, and weather of the Holy Land. These tangents, often referred to a rabbit holes, are to be avoided in the homily. Yes, certainly some details are vital to a particular story, for example, that sheep will not drink from running water is a detail important to why the Good Shepherd leads them beside still waters. Generally speaking, the devil of boredom and time consumption is in the unnecessary details.

Stories, especially life stories, are very prone to going down rabbit holes, tangents to the story, that while interesting at a cocktail party or around the campfire, merely take up precious time in a homily. Stick to the bare bones of a story until you get to your main point. For example, if you want to tell us about the time your father took you to the lake when you were ten years old and the experience that happened there, that's all we need. We don't need to know exactly where the lake is, how long it took to drive there, what route you took. We don't need to know that maybe you weren't ten, but actually eleven, now that you think about it. What happened at the lake? Get to the reason for telling the story. Time is very limited in homily; make good use of it. Don't wander, roam, or stray from what is important; don't get lost in the details.

The State of Affairs in Homily

The General: We are all well aware of the state of the world. We come to Mass in search of the answer to our messy world, complicated country, disruptive community, dysfunctional family life, and/or our own individual chaos. Please spare us the state of the union address. Briefly pointing to it is understandable but badgering us with the litany of the woes of the world is unacceptable; we understand full well that the world is going to hell in a handbasket. We understand that everyone else slept in this morning, but we didn't; hello, we got up and dressed and got ourselves here. Please preach to us and not those still at home in bed. We are here for formation and inspiration, not depression. We come for hope, not despair. The litany of hopelessness is killing us. Enough with all the statistics of the demise of the family, the Church, and the culture. We come to the Table of the Lord, the Mass, in order to worship and to be fed. Enough with the homily that begins by outlining the ills of mankind. Give us hope not despair, mystery not misery.

The Specific: This does not mean that a local or national tragedy that has just occurred is to be ignored. On the contrary, the death of a child in the community, a shooting at a local business, a catastrophic plane crash, or the death of a major political or religious leader in the world <u>ought</u> to be mentioned and in some compassionate manner addressed, *not ignored*, in your homily. The rule of thumb is that if you know full well that everyone is thinking about X, then you must mention X in your homily. You don't want to have parishioners leave Mass wondering what is so wrong with you that you are oblivious to the tragedy that weighs down their hearts.

The Cultural: Know what's going on in the culture, the signs of the times. "Preachers should be aware, in an appropriate way, of what their people are watching on television, what kind of music they are listening to, which websites they find appealing, and which films they find compelling. References to these more popular cultural expressions—which at times can be surprisingly replete with religious motifs—can be an effective way to engage the interest of those on the edge of faith."[14]

Repetition in Homily

The Gospel: Please do not repeat the Gospel reading! We just heard it! It is usually a story, which is basically easy to retain for a short time. Many a homilist is tempted to use the repetition of the gospel story as filler material for the first several minutes or more of the homily. Don't. It is insulting, boring, and aggravating to have to hear it again in the same Mass. The homily is not meant to be an echo of the readings but to expound in some meaningful way upon one or more of them. If your lectors are properly prepared, then your listeners will have heard enough of the readings. I have, on numerous occasions, endured the entire story of the Prodigal Son, which is one of the longest of gospel readings, completely reiterated in the homily, to the utter dismay of the congregation who just survived the reading of the story.

Your Main Point: Whatever the main point of your homily is, please know it and repeat it. The most important point of your homily should be able to be completely stated in one sentence. We should find it in the beginning, middle, and

---

[14] *Preaching the Mystery of Faith: The Sunday Homily,* Committee on Clergy, Consecrated Life, and Vocations, USCCB approved 2012.

conclusion of your homily. It is the ribbon that winds its way through your homily, and which in the end can be tugged in order to tie the homily snuggly together as a drawstring bag is pulled together by a ribbon. Search for the ribbon; every well-constructed homily has one. You create it, repeat it, and draw it tight in closure. It may be a word, a phrase, a sentence; whichever it is, it is to be <u>emphasized</u>, *highlighted*, such that it cannot be missed by the listener. It is almost impossible to remember a homily that does not have a ribbon.

Quotations: Quotations in homily need a particular form of repetition that is difficult at first for some to learn, but comes like any skill, with practice. I refer students to the online spoken poetry of poet David Whyte to learn it well. While you may or may not appreciate the content of his poetry, become familiar with his use of repetition as it will serve you well. When you include a quote in homily, your voice automatically goes into a *high-speed quotation reading cadence* that leaves most listeners hearing words without grasping meaning. When we hear a reader go into this *high-speed quotation reading cadence*, we know it immediately, and some part of our listening brain shuts off. Let's take a look at how to actually do this. Let's say that you choose to use the following rather long quote by the author Henri Nouwen in your homily:

"One of the experiences of prayer is that it seems that nothing happens. But when you start with it and look back over a long period of prayer, you suddenly realize that something has happened. What is most close, most intimate, most present, often cannot be experienced directly but only with a certain distance. When I think I am only distracted, just wasting my time, something is happening too immediate for knowing, understanding, and experiencing. Only in retrospect do I realize that something very important has taken place."[15]

Three things need to happen in order for your listener to actually hear and understand the meaning of the quotation, rather than merely picking up sound vibrations of *blah, blah, blah.* First, you need to train your voice not to go into *high-speed quotation reading cadence*; this is a matter of recognizing it and practicing not doing it. Second, you need the use of repetition within the quotation, and third, the use of emphasis on particular words (below in bold) that help demand the listeners attention. In the homily, this particular quotation would be transformed something akin to this:

"One of the experiences of prayer, /One of the **experiences of prayer**/ is that it seems that nothing happens, /it seems that **nothing happens**/. But when you start with it and look back /**and look back**/ over a long period of prayer / a **long** period of prayer/, you suddenly realize that something has happened / something **has** happened/. What is **most** close, **most** intimate, **most** present, often cannot be

---

[15] Henri J. M. Nouwen "You are the Beloved: Daily Meditations for Spiritual Living," Hachette, UK, 2017.

experienced directly but **only** with a certain distance. When I think I am only distracted, just wasting my time / **just** wasting my time/ something **is** happening too immediate for knowing, understanding, and experiencing. Only in retrospect do I realize that something very important has taken place. /Only in retrospect, **only in retrospect**, do I realize that something **very important** has taken place."

Change in auto-voice cadence, use of internal repetition (rather than repeating the entire quote), and accentuation of appropriate important words will be necessary if you want to use a longer quotation and have it heard. Otherwise, as my father was fond of saying, it will go in one ear and out the other. Shorter quotations will require less repetition, but all require some. Even a one-line quotation will need to be repeated unless it is a well-known quote like "*There but for the grace of God go I.*" A short unknown quote such as "*The eyes are useless if the mind is blind.*" unless repeated, will leave listeners going *Huh? What was that again? I didn't catch that.*

This manner of repetition is certainly not limited to quotations. It can be used as well within the body of your homily to emphasize what you want most noticed and remembered. The whole idea is to get the homily home, to get the homily from the church to the domestic church. If your homily doesn't make it out of the parking lot after Mass, then it has failed. Remember our earlier story of the one egg; the use of repetition is a means to get the egg home, cooked and eaten.

If the homily ends when you stop speaking, there is a problem.

When giving quotation references, use only the author's name, the book if well-known may be mentioned, no page or chapter numbers please. Do not go into source detail in the homily. Especially in reference to biblical quotes, do not mention chapter and verse numbers; these only bog down the spoken word of the homily. *As David reminds us in the Psalms, the Lord is our Shepherd, the Lord is our Shepherd.* Or perhaps you refute *Shakespeare's MacBeth who tells us that our life is a tale full of sound and fury, signifying nothing, signifying nothing.* In any case, go light on reference details in the spoken word as they hinder the ear.

Asking Questions in Homily

Asking questions is always a wonderful way of engaging others and getting to know others. I often employ this tactic at picnics and the occasional cocktail party when I don't know everyone present. *So do you live in the area? What do you do for work? Do you have children?* Questions help people engage and reveal themselves. People also love questions in the form of trivia games and TV game shows as a means of revealing their knowledge of sports, films, history, current events, and the physical world. In other words, questions can be a quite delightful means of engaging one another. So let's take a look at the use of questions in the homily, pros and cons, and possible pitfalls to avoid:

The Question for which you don't want an answer. This falls into two categories:

The Rhetorical Question: The quick rhetorical question can be used as a literary tool, so that instead of saying that *we all want to be happy*, you engage with the question, *don't we all want to be happy?* This kind of simple question doesn't really call for an answer as the answer is inherent in the question.

The I Don't Really Want to Know Your Answer Question: But now let's take a look at a rather more complicated version of the above question concerning happiness. Let's suppose you ask the question *What does it take to make you happy?* This is a deeper, more personal, more intricate question that does not have the generic answer of *yes!* It is fine tuned to the individual, although it certainly will have general references such as lifelong friendships, good health, decent employment, clarity of vocation, a blessed marriage, and perhaps, happy principled children. The answer to this question requires time and thought. I refer here to the story of the negligent hurried roommate. Imagine you have a roommate. One day he runs through the living room in which you are sitting and yells "I'm headed to the grocery store; do you need me to pick up anything for you?!" But before you can think, speak, or in any way respond, he runs to the front door, flies out with the door slamming behind him, jumps into his car and drives away. You are left sitting there wondering why he bothered to ask the question in the first place and certainly knowing that your answer didn't really matter to him.

What does it take to make you happy? If you ask a question that really matters, please give your listeners the opportunity to give themselves an internal second or two to answer it. Ask it again, so they have time to think about it. Do not run out on the question and slam the door behind you. Sometimes, you are tempted to run from the question merely because you believe you don't have time for the answer. Make the time. If you have time for the question, make time for the answer. Three seconds of silence will help the question in your homily be heard. Repeat the question and then take the second or two of silence. Look around. Questions are a great place for glancing un-sustained eye contact. (I say un-sustained, lest your eye contact make any one individual think you expect a verbal public answer from them!)

However, sometimes you are tempted to run from the question because the question consciously or subconsciously frightens you; you find the question too intimate, too deep, too close for comfort, perhaps even too painful to confront. *What does it take to make you happy?* Rule of thumb: never ask a question if you can't handle a moment of silence after asking it. If you are not ready for the answer yourself, don't ask the question of others in your homily.

The Wrong Answer, Funny Answer, Inappropriate answer, or No answer at all:

All of these are pitfalls of asking the non-rhetorical question. These often happen in homilies directed to children in a children's or family Mass, but I've seen it at a regular Sunday Mass as well. Usually, you can get away with a question like *Who built the Ark?* This is because the story of Noah, the animals, and the flood, has filtered down into cultural stories and memorabilia of which those both inside and outside the Church are familiar. Christmas stories are also part of the general culture so a question like *Where did Mary and Joseph put the Baby Jesus when He was born?* will likely get an answer closely connected to mangers and stables. But ask a question like *Who brought the stone tablets down from Mt Sinai?* and already you are on dangerous ground. Make sure you are prepared for the wrong answer, the funny answer, the inappropriate answer, or no answer at all. If you assume that you will get the right answer, and your homily depends on getting that right answer in order for you to smoothly transition to the point of your question, you may well find yourself flailing to regain your composure and struggling for transition.

Some questions are more prone to problematic answers than others. Back in the 1940s, there was a radio show that in the 1950s became a TV show called *Kids Say the Darndest Things* hosted by a gentleman named Art Linkletter. Mr. Linkletter had fine-tuned the art of asking problematic questions to children in order to generate entertaining answers and thereby create a hilarious show. You want to fine tune the opposite art for homily. Ask questions not likely to be problematic and, in any case, prepare for the problematic answer, just to be on the safe side, and be prepared to answer your own question, which rarely goes smoothly. Also, be careful not to fall into the trap of taking too many wrong answers before you answer it yourself. *Who brought the stone tablets down from Mt Sinai? No, not Joseph, no not Noah, no not Jesus, no not Adam...*you see how bad this can get.

The Use of Your Gifts in Homily

What are your personal gifts/abilities, and how can you learn to use them in the homily? This is no time to be shy or reticent; knowing what your gifts are is an honest assessment of what God has given you and is not arrogance but true humility to recognize them and prudence to make use of them. Do not hide your gifts and abilities under the proverbial basket. Use them for the glory of God and the well-being of others. Personal gifts and abilities are best viewed as a spice that can on occasion be added to the main meal; it does not overwhelm the meal, but gently flavors the occasional stew. This subtle flavor can be serious or playful but must always be meaningful. They are not fluff, filler, or superfluous, rather they add something expressive and significant. Here are a few examples of gifts and abilities that I have seen used well in homily; this list is by no means meant to be complete:

Musical Talent: If you have a beautiful voice, please use it on occasion. I heard a homily once where the ribbon of the homily was sung by a deacon who had a voice like an angel: *The Lord is my shepherd, there is nothing I shall want.* It was gentle, yet stunning, heart wrenching, melodious, beautiful, and as the homily came to a close, we were tenderly invited to sing it with him *The Lord is my shepherd, there is nothing I shall want.* This is <u>not</u> an invitation to become the inane Singing Priest, but to accent your homily on appropriate occasions with your talent.

Humor Talent: If you have the natural ability to be funny, to find humor, please make us laugh on occasion. A sense of humor can a times make the unbearable bearable. Many a painful funeral has been lifted to a higher plane by a light story, a laugh at our human frailty, a memorable amusement that touches the heart. Please be clear that I am not referring to useless jokes or stories that turn the Mass into a comedy club. All humor in homily must first and foremost reflect that the homily is part of the Mass and never lose sight of this. As we live in a culture where humor is out of control, crass, often inappropriate, and commonly obscene, we must guard the use of humor diligently. That being said, if humor is your gift, please find meaningful ways to use it in your homilies

Native Language/Culture Talent: If English is your second language and the United States is your second culture, please don't hide your first language and culture. There are so many language and cultural delights that can be added to your homily if you have a different heritage from the community you serve. People of good will are naturally curious about your background, especially if different from their own. Share your language, culture, food concepts, music; pray about ways to incorporate the life in which you were born into your homily. For example, if Spanish is your first language, do not be afraid to begin your homily on Good Shepherd Sunday with "Jesus is our good shepherd, la pastora, our pastor, la pastora, who shepherds our hearts…" (Notice that you do not need to mention that this is how to say it 'in Spanish', just roll it in casually!) In this way you incorporate the familiarity of your native language into your homily, helping both yourself and your new community come together in this intimacy of personal communication. Discuss with your congregation in bits and pieces the traditions, rituals, foods, music, and language that has shaped and enhanced your life experience and that you carry still in your heart. Pour your authentic roots into your second language and culture and allow it to flower in new ways in your homily.

Flaws as Gifts: If you have a particular flaw (I am not referring to vices or sins!), bring this flaw into the light when appropriate in homily. Sharing your humanity is a great method of communication, manner of humility, and leads often to a sense of humor over our shared human frailty. I suffer from prosopagnosia, commonly called face blindness; I cannot recognize faces at all. I recognize people by their hair style, clothing, and context, which can all vary greatly. I used to try to hide this fact which led to many embarrassing and problematic encounters. Now when I meet people, I tell them right off the bat that if I run into them tomorrow at the supermarket, I won't know them from Adam. They are still surprised when it happens, but no longer confused, hurt, or angry by being ignored when I don't show any sign of recognition, rather they come to me and remind me who they are! So, if you have a problem like an inability to remember faces, names, dates, if you have a stutter, are deaf in one ear, have a physical disability, are tone deaf and can't sing a note, or some other issue that is not going to go away, please say so. If your problem or issue might in any way interfere with your ability to serve, because it is unknown or misunderstood, bring it into the light with your congregation in some charming, organic way, in your homily. The words of poet David Whyte come to mind: *"If only our own faces would allow the invisible carver's hand to bring the deep grain of love to the surface. If only we knew as the carver knew, how the flaws in the wood led his searching chisel to the very core, we would smile too and not need faces immobilized by fear and the weight of things undone."*[16] Do not be immobilized by your flaws; see them as gifts that God has allowed for some greater good. Prayerfully search for how they are to be brought to the light and used in homily in order to better serve your community.

Current Events in Homily

Politics: Pope Benedict XVI stated: "The Church wishes to help form consciences in political life and to stimulate greater insight into the authentic requirements of justice as well as greater readiness to act accordingly, even when this might involve conflict with situations of personal interest... The Church cannot and must not take upon herself the political battle to bring about the most just society possible. She cannot and must not replace the State. Yet at the same time she cannot and must not remain on the sidelines in the fight for justice."[17] There is a fine line between taking a moral stand on issues within politics and taking a political stand on a particular political party or candidate. Remembering once again the place of the homily within the Mass, one must take care not to turn the Mass into a political podium. There is a

---

[16]David Whyte, *Close to Home*, Ish River Productions, CD, 1992.

[17] Pope Benedict XVI, Deus Caritas Est, 28, 2005.

huge difference between saying: you must vote for Candidate X of Political Party X because they are pro-life and saying: we are obligated as Catholics to understand the importance of the abortion issue and the sacredness of all life, especially a baby in the womb, and the Church directs us to vote accordingly on this issue of extreme moral importance of our day. That being said, the Church recognizes that one may in good conscience approach issues of moral significance in various and nuanced ways. Once again, I highly recommend that you read *Forming Consciences for Faithful Citizenship - Part I - The U.S. Bishops' Reflection on Catholic Teaching and Political Life.* In it we are reminded that "The Church is involved in the political process but is not partisan. The Church cannot champion any candidate or party...The Church is principled but not ideological."

Major events/Tragedies: Tragedies of which most everyone is aware, be they world, national, local, or within the Church parish family are to be recognized in the next possible homily or homilies over the week or weekend. Do not ignore tragedies that are on most everyone's mind and heart. For many years, I watched very little television, but I did turn it on for five major events: The Fall of the Berlin Wall, the Space Shuttle Challenger blowing up, and the World Trade Centers' horror on 9/11, the death of Saint Mother Teresa of Calcutta, and the death of Pope John Paul II. Certain events are not to be ignored. This is true within the homily as well. Do not try to ignore what everyone is thinking about like the proverbial elephant in the room. This includes local disasters such as a deadly tornado, a school shooting, and closer to home, the death of a child in the parish family. Tragedies come to mind more than great joyous events, but certainly the election of a new Pope, for example, would be a joyous Church and world event to be noted in the upcoming homily.

To touch on these matters of great significance, even briefly, is to show that you are aware of what affects the lives of those whom you serve, that you care about what affects them, and that you rejoice or commiserate with them. You are not oblivious. You hold their hearts in your heart. "The true pastor and good shepherd knows his people's sorrows, their anxieties, their weaknesses, their capacity for love, their abiding joys, and their deepest longings. Only when the homilist, in a spirit of faith and love, is conscious of his own deepest experience and those of his people can he preach persuasively to them."[18] If a particular tragedy is so bad that you are at a loss for how to deal with it, if words fail you, tell your parishioners that; turn perhaps to a moment of silence. In some way, show that you care.

---

[18] *Preaching the Mystery of Faith: The Sunday Homily,* Committee on Clergy, Consecrated Life, and Vocations, USCCB approved 2012.

The Use of the Readings in Homily

You have at least three readings for every daily Mass: The Old Testament reading, the Psalm, and the Gospel reading. On feasts and Sundays, you have an additional reading from the New Testament put in for good measure giving you a total of four readings every week from which to derive a basis for your homily. Why would you think that you need any additional biblical material for your homily? Stick with the readings you have been given! The occasional reference to another reading, parable, connection is fine, but don't go off on a tangent of other readings with which you are more comfortable. We have all heard homilies that begin with one gospel reading and end with a completely different gospel reading because...why? Because the homilist went down a rabbit hole, a pointless digression, that's why!

There is no need to incorporate all three or four readings into your homily. Sometimes there is a clear theme that runs through all the readings, and sometimes there is not. Don't turn yourself inside out trying to make connections that aren't really there, and please don't give three or four separate mini-homilies on each reading demanding that we jump from pillar to post along with you. Through prayer, find what the Holy Spirit tells you is important to speak about this time, to these people. We understand that you have a thousand ideas and that you are longing to cram them all into a ten-minute homily, but that desire needs to be set aside. The homily demands that you focus on a particular goal, the one egg, in order that the homily make it home. Keep in mind always, however, that "it is common knowledge that among all the Scriptures, even those of the New Testament, the Gospels have a special preeminence, and rightly so, for they are the principal witness for the life and teaching of the incarnate Word, our savior."[19]

We might also note here that all references to Scripture need <u>not</u> include chapter and verse numbers. Therefore, it suffices to say that *Paul told the Corinthians that the foolishness of God is wiser than man's wisdom,* without chapter and verse numbers mentioned and which would only bog down the flow of thought.

Also, lest there be any confusion, know that "*the readings drawn from sacred Scripture may never be replaced by other texts,* however significant the latter may be from a spiritual or pastoral standpoint: 'No text of spirituality or literature can equal the value and riches contained in sacred Scripture, which is the word of God'."[20] You may certainly use other sources in your homily, but these other pieces of literature may never *replace* the readings from sacred Scripture.

---

[19] *Dei Verbum*, 18.
[20] *Dei Verbum* 69.

The Use of Resources in Homily

There are many resources for homiletic material beginning with your theological education, your life experience, cultural references, literature, music, the world of art in its many forms. There is your inspiration from your prayer life and your *Lectio Divina* meditations.

The internet now gives access to endless concepts and ideas. This can be both a good thing and a menace. An endless multitude of homilies, written by other priests for other times, places, and congregations, can be a great source of inspiration for ideas, but can also now be merely downloaded, stolen, and repeated. This latter sad practice goes against everything that a homily should be. It also expresses a lack of understanding that the Holy Spirit can speak through you.

A note on theological sources: beware. Stick to sources approved by the Church and be wary of concepts introduced in other sources that appear to be in conflict with official Church teachings or that seem a bit off or odd. There are so many amazing Church documents available for your consideration as resources for homilies, such as papal letters and encyclicals and books from solid members of the Church; theological concepts are best gleaned from these and not questionable or dubious theological sources.

These controversial sources include ideas pulled from *unapproved apparitions* or yet to be approved apparitions of Our Lady; be careful. I recently heard a homily in which the priest said that Mary said something really surprising in an unapproved apparition and then he repeated, in the homily, this very odd idea, which was not just peculiar, but highly suspect. Speculation does not belong in a homily. The homily is not the place for any theological conjecture, guesswork, dissension, or confusion.

Facts and Fictions in the Homily

Aside from theological assertions within the homily, that clearly ought to be known, understood, and in line with Church teaching, there will be other statements from science, literature, and the world in general that, when used in your homily, ought also, to the best of your knowledge, be in line with the truth. Unfortunately, there are three primary categories of knowledge: What you know you know, what you know you don't know, and what you don't know that you don't know—this last category is very problematic. Therefore, if you are referring to something that is outside your normal realm of knowledge, please, check it out! For example, I have heard homilies about sheep drinking from rushing streams (they won't!) and another about salt going saltless in the cupboard (it won't!) The natural habits of sheep and the chemistry of salt were outside the common knowledge of the homilist. Nowadays, a relatively easy google check would ascertain that sheep need to be led beside still waters in order feel safe enough to drink and will die of thirst next to a rushing river. Salt in the Gospel parable loses its flavor because back in the day folks gathered salty sand at the seashore and put it in a small bag which was dipped into the soup pot and this pouch would eventually lose its salty flavor when the salt leached out leaving the sand behind. These are just two simple examples of how the homilist can appear foolish to the farmers and chemists in the congregation, so be on the lookout for such fictions in your homily that you wrongly assume are facts.

Rule of thumb: If it is a subject outside of your general knowledge, please fact check. Furthermore, we live in a world that is constantly in a state of flux; things change, matters develop, issues evolve, devolve, progress and regress. If you are going to discuss a matter in your homily, make sure that you are up to date on the subject at hand. Concerning more sensitive matters keep in mind the old adage, "Fools rush in where angels fear to tread."[21]

"Modern man cannot do without information that is full, consistent, accurate and true. Without it, he cannot understand the perpetually changing world in which he lives nor be able to adapt himself to the real situation. This adaptation calls for frequent decisions that should be made with a full knowledge of events. Only in this way can he assume a responsible and active role in his community and be a part of

---

[21] Alexander Pope, English poet, *An Essay on Criticism*, 1709.

its economic, political, cultural and religious life. With the right to be informed goes the duty to seek information. Information does not simply occur; it has to be sought."[22] "You must continually stand at the window, open to the world; you are obliged to study the facts, the events, the opinions, the current interests, the thought of the surrounding environment."[23]

"Every communication must comply with certain essential requirements, and these are sincerity, honesty and truthfulness. Good intentions and a clear conscience do not thereby make a communication sound and reliable. A communication must state the truth. It must accurately reflect the situation with all its implications. The moral worth and validity of any communication does not lie solely in its theme or intellectual content. The way in which it is presented, the way in which it is spoken and treated and even the audience for which it is designed - all these factors must be taken into account."[24]

---

[22] *"Communio Et Progressio"* On the Means of Social Communication, Part 2, 34. Second Vatican Council, May 23, 1971

[23] Paul VI: Allocution to the Officers of the Catholic Association of Italian Journalists. L'Osservatore Romano, January 24, 1969.

[24] *"Communio Et Progressio"* On the Means of Social Communication, Part 1, 17. Second Vatican Council, May 23, 1971.

Chapter 5

Body Matters

The Present of those Present

Remember that your homily is intended for those who are present (actually or virtually) at this Mass. Often, one is tempted to address derogatory or critical comments <u>to</u> or <u>about</u> those who are *not* present. Rule of thumb: Never speak in any negative manner <u>to</u> or <u>about</u> those who are not present. For one thing, they are not there to defend themselves. For a second, far more serious reason, it is easy to set up a dichotomy of *they/them out there* and *we/us in here*, which very easily digresses to the *sinners out there* and we *holy persons in here*. The dangers of this should be clear. Thirdly, you lose time addressing those who <u>are</u> present, those who managed to get to Mass and await your words for them.

Body Language in Homily

We listen long before you speak. Parishioners watch your every move, particularly at the altar. Do you bow when you cross in front of the altar, do you genuflect to the Tabernacle, do you move with respect and reverence for the space in which you serve? Or do you trot around like you are in a bowling alley? Do you slouch, shuffle, or scurry? Do you yawn? How do you approach the ambo, the pulpit? Are you excited to speak, or bored, or reticent, or a nervous wreck? Do you have confidence in your message, know what you want to convey, or are you timid and unsure? It's generally all there in your body language. Let's take a brief look at a few particulars of body language.

Walking: Walk, do not run. Do not scurry. You are not a squirrel. At a cheap hamburger joint, servers often scurry, but if you have ever been in a fine dining establishment you know that the waiters never ever scurry; rather, they move slowly, with clear purpose, and with elegance. The Mass is the latter, not the former. Never rush unless there is a fire. You set a tone to the Mass by your bodily attention to decorum and a sense of dignity. Therefore, on the other foot, do not shuffle or drag your feet like sleepwalker or zombie; walk like one who is alert to the grace of the moment.

Posture: Do not slouch. Pull your shoulders back in line with your spine. Unless you are elderly or have a physical impediment, please don't drag yourself around the altar like you are an orangutan. I finally asked one of my seminarians, who was apparently unaware of his posture, why he moved around the altar like he was in a cage. Shocked, he responded that he had spent ten years working as a guard in a maximum-security prison and that that posture was taught as the safest posture if attacked by a violent prisoner! Good to know! It took ten minutes for him to learn to walk correctly at the altar once he became aware of the problem.

Does your posture match your words? There are appropriate casual postures of relaxation and funny issues, and there are appropriate serious postures of deeply crucial and painful issues. When these get mixed up, it can be very confusing for your listeners, to say the least. The worst-case scenario is, of course, the casual flippant body language while discussing a grave matter. Keeping your body in synch with your homily takes practice, especially if you are nervous, so you need to be aware of this possible problem.

Eye Contact: Love is an I-Thou relationship that requires eye contact unless both of us are blind. Try speaking to a friend while looking at the wall behind the person; this gets very weird, very fast. We know if you are looking at us or at the back wall. Many a nervous speaker thinks they can get away with little or no eye contact, but this is not the case. In college I once saw a speaker give an entire hour-long lecture to the bowl of popcorn in front of the lectern intended for the after-lecture refreshment; he spoke to the popcorn! Your eyes need to sweep the audience, making direct eye contact. No, you cannot get away with looking at the tops of our heads, either. Try it with a friend. Speak without any eye contact; look at each other's heads. Communication breaks down very quickly. Nor can you look at just one person for the whole homily; nor can you look at any one person for too long. Especially when discussing sins!

So, there is an art to be learned when it comes to eye contact that takes practice. I recommend that if eye contact is difficult for you, that you begin by looking at people that you know well and who are more likely to nod in encouragement or give some form of comfort in their return gaze. I once spoke at the end of Mass concerning our Haiti mission, and I got nothing from the sleepy early Mass parishioners until I glanced upon one teenager nodding to me, obviously excited by the concept I was expounding on; this young man gave me quiet support and the courage to continue my talk with confidence. Look around! If you need practice, round up two or three friends and practice in an otherwise empty church. If you have no friends handy, use puppets, stuffed animals, paintings of saints, magazine photos, any moveable objects placed strategically around the pews, and learn to speak to them directly, making eye contact. You may laugh, but this method works!

Hands: Do you know what they do when you speak? You better, because hands are prone to have a mind of their own! Hands have been known to flail wildly about with every word you speak, jingle change in your pants pockets, frenetically grip the podium as though an earthquake were occurring, scratch heads and other body parts unawares, point fingers menacingly at parishioners, and/or hang limply, reminiscent of the orangutan, at one's side. Pay attention to your hands; if you do not control them, they will control your homily.

Feet: Be aware of tapping, wiggling, rolling, and teetering from side to side. Since your feet are connected to the rest of you and are the foundation of the rest of you, feet often control what your knees, hips, and shoulders are doing. Your feet cannot be doing a dance separate from the homily; become aware of what they are doing.

Tics: These are repetitive abnormal body behaviors or throat vocalizations, usually of which you are unaware. They include things like eye blinking, various body parts moving, throat clearing, coughing, foot shaking or wiggling, nail picking or face picking, and head or hair scratching. We are not concerned here with twitches related to physical problems, but tics related to nervousness when speaking. They are a bodily "go to" when anxious or uncomfortable. Usually, you need someone else to make you aware of these oddities, but aware of them you must become because your audience is most certainly aware of them. A tic can take over a homily. The best way to get over a tic is to first become aware of it and then slowly learn to substitute the tic with a behavior less noticeable. For example, pressing your foot firming into the floor can replace a desire to wiggle the foot uncontrollably; keeping your hands actively on the podium can replace involuntary scratching of your head. More persistent tics will need adverse conditioning such as snapping your wrist with a rubber band for several weeks every time you do it; works quite well. Eventually, you will outgrow the need for these interventions.

Face: The face is the primary means by which we quickly determine if a person is happy or sad, joyful or miserable, alert or exhausted, connected or disconnected. Generally speaking, you want your face to proclaim the good news before you proclaim it in words. Please smile when it is appropriate to do so! Yes, smile; it is the universal language of happiness. I have seen many an Easter, Christmas, Good Shepherd, Christ the King homily delivered like it was still Good Friday. Why should we want what you have if you never smile? I understand that if you are nervous, you will often find it very difficult to muster up a smile, yet a smile can instantly relax your congregation, and surprisingly, relax you, especially when the people of God smile in return. "Every time you smile at someone, it is an action of love, a gift to that person, a beautiful thing."[1]

Voice Matters and Word Emphasis in Homily

My mother was fond of telling me when I was a teenager that it was not *what* I had said but *how* I had said it that infuriated her. *"I don't like your tone of voice, young lady!"* We all intrinsically understand this sentiment. Our tone of voice matters. There are several issues connected with tone of voice to be considered:

---

[1] Saint Mother Teresa of Calcutta, *The Best Gift is Love: Meditations* (Ann Arbor, MI: Servant Books, 1993).

Matching: Does your tone of voice match what you are saying? Have you ever seen a news reporter joyfully discussing a tragedy? Yes, it happens. Five people were mangled in a car accident and the reporter sounds gleeful just because there is something to report. If the emotion in your voice does not match the content of your words, there is a problem of an affective disconnect. If the matter is sorrowful and grave but you sound chipper or if the matter is joyful and you sound miserable, then there is an auditory confusion that undergirds your homily right off the bat. I find this confusion more likely to happen when the matter is serious and sorrowful. It is easier to participate in joy and happiness, towards which we naturally lean. However, I have heard plenty of dismal Christmas and Easter homilies that ought to easily be joyful, one would think. Sorrow, misery, and/or death is even harder to properly connect with. This problem often begins in the readings and carries over to the homily. The matter is grave or sorrowful, but the tone of voice is flippant or disengaged. John the Baptist is beheaded, the disciples retrieve his body, Jesus goes off to pray in the desert, and you don't really sound like you care deeply about this tragedy; your voice doesn't portray that you really get it, understand it, or care. Your tone of voice doesn't match the matter at hand. You are the confused reporter.

Compassion: Does your tone of voice contain love and compassion for the difficulty of the human condition? Can we say that you care about us by the tone of your voice? Or are you arrogant, haughty, or condescending? Does your tone of voice convey that you are in the boat with us? Can you deliver a painful truth with gentle compassion?

Modulation: Does your tone of voice vary? Or is your entire homily delivered in monotone. This monotone can even be one of high-pitched excitement that carries on until everyone listening is exhausted. Does your volume change from loud to soft, up and down, excitement and subdued? Do you always yell or always whisper? Are you stuck in one tone or mode of voice? Do you project or do you mumble? Can you project feeling in your voice that allows us also to feel something vital, without making us feel for you? Can your voice start in one place and carefully direct us to another place by a change in tone, volume, emotion? Or are you tempted to start where you plan to end in order to bypass the journey of homily? When I teach homiletics, every seminarian will sooner or later be asked to give a homily facing the wall, facing away from the listeners. No longer able to rely on body language for expression, the homilist must learn to rely solely on voice intonation, volume, charism. Can you pour your entire body and soul into just your voice? Is your voice believable; is it connected to your heart and intellect? Or are you merely mouthing words?

Emphasis: What is the most important sentence in your homily? What is the most important word in each sentence? If you don't know, neither will your listeners. Let's take a look at one sentence: *Jesus hears your prayers.* This one sentence can have several different meanings depending on which word is emphasized:

Jesus hears your prayers. It's *Jesus* who matters; *He* is the one
   who hears your prayers, not me or your neighbor, *Jesus*!
Jesus *hears* your prayers. Jesus is not just passive, but actively
   hears you! He's *listening* for you to speak. Jesus *acts*!
Jesus hears *your* prayers. Jesus hears not only my prayers, but
   He hears *your* prayers. *Your* personal prayers matter!
Jesus hears your *prayers*. Jesus hears many things, but of pri-
   mary importance to Him are your *prayers*! *Prayer* is vital.

So, when you say the sentence: *Jesus hears your prayers,* which sentence are you saying, which word are you stressing? If you aren't sure, or outright don't know, don't expect your congregation to know either. Every sentence of the homily must be clearly understood by you, or the entire homily becomes wishy washy and/or confusing to those listening to it. This is accomplished through your inflection, nuance, and accentuation.

Verbal Tics: These are not the throat vocalization tics referred to above, but verbal tics, of which most people are also unaware. These include using words such as "like" and "ya know" in every sentence, as well as *humming* and/or *umming/ahhing* between sentences, repeatedly. One winds up with sentences such as "Jesus is, like, ya know, um, the Second Person of the, um, Trinity. He was born in, um,

Bethlehem to a woman betrothed, um, to a man named Joseph, ya know." After three sentences like this the listener is ready to smack their forehead or yours. Verbal tics may be the hardest to get rid of because you cannot really replace them with another behavior as you can with bodily tics. You must become aware of them in your speech patterns and then practice saying sentences without them. Practice saying "It is raining outside today" to replace "It is, like, um, raining outside today.

There is also what I prefer to call the "verbal tics of relativism." These are usually best expressed by beginning every sentence or concrete idea with the words "for me" or ending every thought with "to me." The words "to/for me" have the power to negate every concept of objectivity and universality of truth, goodness, and beauty. It is deeply connected to the false notion that "beauty is in the eye of the beholder." It is not. The sunset is objectively beautiful; if you subjectively fail to recognize this, the problem is not in the beauty of the sunset but in you; the beauty is there regardless of your soul's eye's ability to see it. The Eucharist is the source and summit of the Christian faith, *to me*. No, *not to me*, to and for all, whether recognized or not. When you qualify universal truths with *to/for me* you dilute, relativize, privatize, and weaken their significance. These words of subjectivity are often used either without realization or with a false sense of tolerance, sensibility, and political correctness or out of fear of speaking the truth as truth. Become aware of your use of these words that invalidate the objectivity of truth, goodness, and beauty. Relegate them to the realm of the truly subjective, if you must use them: Chocolate ice cream is the best flavor in the world, to me. But be aware that even this is objectively true, for to me it is.

Universals: Be very careful with your use of words that assume universality where it may not actually exist: all, everyone, everywhere, always, at all times, never, no one, nobody, nothing, and other references to universality. *Everyone loves to go to the beach.* Well, I don't because my son drowned last year, I have eczema and burn to a crisp, or I can't swim and I'm afraid of sharks. Far better to say: *Many of us love to go to the beach.* Another area where it is easy to fall into universal traps is with statements like: *Killing is always wrong.* The war veteran who defended the country is going to take issue, to say the least. Our theology is highly defined, and we understand that murder is always wrong but killing is not. Be careful with those universals.

Assumptions: Be on the lookout for assumptions in your homily. One of the most distressing assumptions that I see frequently in homily is the assumption that everyone had a happy childhood, with a good mother and a good father. This is not merely an incorrect assumption but a painful one to many in your flock. Many people are survivors of extremely dysfunctional homes of addiction, absent parents, emotionally or physically abusive parents, hostile environments. How blessed you are if your childhood was good, loving, and led you to the priesthood. But do not assume that this is a universal state of affairs; it is not. Other assumptions also abound such as the moral beliefs that no one in your parish has committed major fraud, adultery, murder, or had an abortion. Assumptions can also include incorrect opinions that everyone in the congregation has the basic necessities of life such as food, shelter, proper clothing, education. The more you get to know the people you serve, the less likely you are to make false assumptions. In the meantime, be careful.

Volume: It is important that you can be heard. Most churches today have fairly good to excellent sound systems. However, many a speaker simply does not understand how a microphone works; it requires your cooperation. "The biggest error is failing to project one's voice, something that requires opening one's mouth, breathing from the diaphragm, lifting up one's voice, and sending it out. Speech teachers say you should throw your voice against the back wall. This is not the same as yelling,"[2] and therefore practice is required to understand how well your sound system functions, the degree to which you must project your voice, and the difference between yelling and projecting.

---

[2] Alfred McBride, O.Praem., *How to Make Homilies Better, Briefer, Bolder* (Huntington, IN: Our Sunday Visitor, Inc., 2007), p. 123.

Speed: Once you are at the pulpit, own the moment. Do not speed speak; slow down. Nerves usually make one speak more quickly, so become aware of this. "Take it easy and don't rush. The bigger your church, the more you need to slow down, let the sound (and the meaning) reach the ears and minds of your people."[3]

Your Invisibility Cloak in Homily

In a truly great performance, you no longer see the performer performing. Rather you see that to which the entire performance points. Think of a film or live play; to the extent that you see the actor rather than the character portrayed, the actor has failed. To the extent that you see the character rather than the actor, the actor has succeeded. I once knew a genuinely great puppeteer who, when he performed with a puppet, you lost all sight of him and only saw the character of the puppet. However, after the show, children and parents did not want to talk to him, they only wanted to talk to the puppet! He found this too difficult to handle personally and left puppeteering. This was a shame because his invisibility was what made him great. Your homily must contain this personal invisibility which allows your homily to point to

---

[3] Alfred McBride, O.Praem., *How to Make Homilies Better, Briefer, Bolder.* (Huntington, IN: Our Sunday Visitor, Inc., 2007), p.124.

Jesus, not to you. "Be careful with every homily. They want to hear Jesus, not you; only Jesus, always Jesus."[4] When your homily is over, your listeners should want to talk more to Jesus than to you. Invisibility is closely linked to humility, confidence, and an understanding that your life is not about you, but about being a gift for others.

Do not confuse invisibility with being impersonal. Rather it is a radical personability that is not self-seeking but other seeking that allows for invisibility to happen. Picture a person with a flashlight walking with you in a dark wood. If he shines the light on himself, neither of you can see anything but his face. If he shines the light away from himself to the pathway, you cannot see him, but both of you can journey safely through the lighted woods. Invisibility in homily allows you to point the light towards the path rather than towards yourself.

Do not confuse performance with "performing" in its negative connotation. In genuine performance art, there is a heart-engaged authenticity that "performing" lacks. Authenticity comes from the intellect and through the heart; "performing" comes only from the intellect. When the mind, bypassing the heart, tries to force a concept into speech it becomes an oddly false version of what it is meant to be. "Performing" that is overburdened with artificial and exag-

---

[4] Lingayen-Dagupan Archbishop Socrates Villegas at the Cathedral of Lingayen-Dagupan, April 2, 2015.

gerated emotion, exaggerated caricature versions of reality, becomes embarrassing for the performer and extremely uncomfortable for the audience. We have all experienced this kind of affective speaking that is either melodramatic, condescending, or oddly emotive, and which leaves us cringing. Learning true performance art is to return to authentic art, art as an external image of beauty, goodness, and truth that is a marriage of intellect and heart. A homily, as well as the prior proclaiming of Holy Scripture, ought never be "performed." Rather, homily is an authentic art form of genuine communication that arises from and through the heart after true understanding has been reached by the intellect.

The Use of Props in Homily

As much as I hate to bring up the use of props, it must be dealt with because so many people either love them or hate them. So, let's begin by recalling that the homily is part of the Mass, so any props must be considered and accepted or rejected in light of that fact. Therefore, props that do not distract from the solemnity of the Mass can be used, especially for children and family Masses. I recommend the old KISS rule of Keep It Simple. Needless to say, this leaves out hover boards zooming through the church, clowns appearing at the pulpit, convoluted antics, chemistry experiments, and/or elaborate character costume changes during the homily. Simple things like a pair of sunglasses that come and go, a crown for a king, a cell phone to point to technology, the lighting of a candle, a book or painting held up to make a clear reference, these short-lived showings of a minor prop are acceptable *occasionally*; make sure that your parishioners are not awaiting your weekly homiletic prop.

Keep in mind that you and your prop may well forever be remembered, for better or for worse. A prop can work well if it reflects your personality, and it will fail miserably if it does not reflect some aspect of the inner you. Either way, it will stick to you like glue because it tells us something by your having chosen it. Spock was the well-known *Star Trek* character played by Leonard Nimoy. For years after the series ended, Nimoy tried to shake off the character, even going so far as to write a book in 1975 entitled *I Am Not Spock*. Twenty years later, Nimoy wrote *I Am Spock*, realizing that there was no escape from this image he had embraced. So, choose your props carefully, cautiously, thoughtfully, for you may find yourself wedded to it, for better or for worse.

Where is the line between charming and foolish? To begin with, let us understand that these are not merely subjective matters, but objective black and white realities. If your prop idea is anywhere near the gray zone, forget it. When in doubt, don't. Your bad idea will never be forgotten, will get you an invite to visit the bishop, and might even grant you regrettable press and social media coverage. A good rule of thumb concerning children and family Masses is that if a prop would be unacceptable at a regular Mass, it is probably also unacceptable at a special Mass. The presence of children is not a reason to turn the Mass into a parody.

All that being said, simple props can be delightful, insightful, and memorable. We are not Manichean; we view the material world as good, and the Church certainly embraces stuff. We must just be aware that some stuff more easily lends itself to the secular than to the sacred.

Chapter 6

Spirit Matters

The Use of Silence in the Homily

Silence is the medium in which words exist. It is the landscape in which we pray. The poet Rumi tells us that *"the quieter we are the more we are able to hear."*[1] Emily Dickenson tells us that *"saying nothing sometimes says the most."*[2] We are often told that *silence is golden.* Author Robert Sardello, refers to silence as a *"companion-presence"* that is not *"a mere absence of sound."*[3] St. John Paul II understood the greatest mystery of silence and revealed that *"In this silence of the white Host, carried in the Monstrance, are all His words; there is His whole life given in offering to the Father for each of us..."*[4] All His words are carried in the Great Silence.

"In the course of the homily, the hearts of believers keep silence and allow God to speak. The Lord and his people speak to one another in a thousand ways directly, without intermediaries. But in the homily they want someone to

---

[1] Poet Rumi, 13th century mystic. www.goodreads.com, 2021.

[2] Emily Dickenson, letter to her aunt, 1874.

[3] Robert Sardello, *Silence: The Mystery of Wholeness* (Benson, NC: Goldenstone Press, 2006).

[4] Pope John Paul II, Angelus,(1) June 17, 1979.

serve as an instrument and to express their feelings in such a way that afterwards, each one may chose how he or she will continue the conversation."[5] To be this instrument, you, too, must embrace an inner silence.

And so now we ask the question, how comfortable are you with silence? Can you sit still and pray in it? Do you fear it or are you friends with it? Can you enter in as into a landscape? Can you enter into great silence as Person? Can you ask a question or present an idea and then remain silent? Or must you rush forward and fill the silence with speech? Your comfort level with silence will be reflected in two ways, that are in fact two sides of the same penny, so to speak: Your comfort level with silence will be reflected in 1) your ability to speak and 2) your ability to know when not to speak and actively enter into silence. This is an understanding of silence as an action, not merely the passive lack of speaking.

Silence is the only medium in which we can reflect, contemplate, understand, discover, and recover. Both external silence and internal silence allow for the growth of wisdom. Can you ask a question or present an idea in the homily and then be silent? Can you allow your question or your concept time to sink in? *Mary and Joseph have arrived in Bethlehem seeking shelter and now there is no room at the inn. Why is there no room at the inn? Why do we have no place in our lives*

---

[5] *Evangelii Gaudium*, 143.

for the Baby Jesus? Can you ask this question and then be silent? Listen for a pin to drop. Can you allow Silence itself to do its own work? The Silence is there in the Blessed Sacrament, quite near to you as you give your homily; can you allow this great Silence to do its own mysterious work? Ah, but it is so hard to be silent! Shhhhhh. Listen. Enter in to the great and holy Silence.

"In their interventions, a good number of Synod Fathers insisted on the importance of silence in relation to the word of God and its reception in the lives of the faithful. The word, in fact, can only be spoken and heard in silence, outward and inward. Ours is not an age which fosters recollection; at times one has the impression that people are afraid of detaching themselves, even for a moment, from the mass media. For this reason, it is necessary nowadays that the People of God be educated in the value of silence. Rediscovering the centrality of God's word in the life of the Church also means rediscovering a sense of recollection and inner repose. The great patristic tradition teaches us that the mysteries of Christ all involve silence. Only in silence can the word of God find a home in us, as it did in Mary, woman of the word and, inseparably, woman of silence. Our liturgies must facilitate this attitude of authentic listening: *Verbo crescente, verba deficiunt.*"[6]

---

[6] *Verbum Domini*, 66.

Silence is an art to be learned. Silence is a landscape to become familiar with. Silence is a language of love to be sought. In the homily it is reflected in mere seconds, but those seconds matter more than words can say. Go easy on yourself and find gentle ways to slowly incorporate silence into your homily. You may well find silence very uncomfortable at first; do not let this discomfort dismay you. Silence is deeply powerful, and its use in your homily will come at the price of your submission to it. This can be a painful transition for many, but it's worth the work, for silence is golden.

Into The Deep of the Homily

This concept is closely related to the one above concerning silence. Often it is difficult to handle silence, but it can be as difficult to handle words. Can you speak deep words, tackle intimacy, ask painful questions and in a true sense, *own them*? *Own them* in the understanding that they are yours, spoken from your mouth, poured from your heart? Or do they scare you? Have you exposed more of your inner being, your soul, than you are prepared to reveal? Intimacy requires groundwork, foundation, inner strength, preparation of body, mind, and soul.

I once heard an amazing storyteller tell a heart wrenching story about slavery. In the story, the slaves, men, women, and children, had escaped and were making their way on a difficult journey toward freedom. As they neared the sea, they were ambushed by their would-be captors. Having to choose between a return to captivity or drowning in the sea, they chose the latter. Hand in hand they walked into the arms of the deadly sea as together they sang an ancient ancestral song. The storyteller, who had a deep melodious voice, sang for us this song from her own ancestral background, and together our souls walked into the sea. The audience was deeply and intimately enmeshed in the story; it was soul haunting. We were stunned by the intensity of the entire experience. Then without missing a beat, the storyteller came out of the song, shrugged her shoulders, laughed, and said in a most flippant voice "But I don't know if this story is true or not, who knows." We were hurled out of the experience unto the harsh sand of a different reality. This was a storyteller who couldn't own the pain, intimacy, depth, fragility, of her own story. She wanted to tell it, but wasn't prepared to tell it.

When Christ asks Peter to *"put out into the deep water,"*[7] Peter considers his level of faith in Jesus and decides, by grace, to do so. This is a pivotal moment; without this affirmative decision there will be no catch. It is no different with you. The intimacy and depth of the effective homily requires your affirmative decision to *put out into the deep.* Notice that Peter refers to Jesus as *"Master"*[8] when he is told to put out

---

[7] NRSVCE, John 5:4.
[8] NRSVCE, John 5:5.

into the deep and lower his nets for a catch. This is a level of intimate faith that demands that you too know the Master. Furthermore, note that Peter has *the skills* necessary to put out into the deep water. Never tackle a deep issue, story, or concept that you are in some way unprepared to handle. Peter puts out into the deep with sincere faith, tender submission, and essential skill.

If you can't yet own your words, please don't speak them in your homily. A good check for this is if you are tempted in any way to move quickly from the serious to the flippant, the deep to the joke, the silence to the laugh, from the solemn to the folly, from the holy to the hoot, as well as physical fidgeting and nervous impulses. Become aware of these signs, red flags, that you need to wait until you are better prepared by work and grace to put out into the deep.

Intimacy in the Homily

Intimacy is integral to the homily. We preach a God who knows us intimately, knits us together in secret, calls us by name, holds us in the palm of His hand, pours out His Blood for us, searches us out when we are lost, rejoices at our homecoming. This is not a distant, aloof, reserved, indifferent being in a galaxy far far away. No, rather this God is willing to become Incarnate, take on our nature, live amongst us, weep with us, touch our disease, spit on our tongue, stick his fingers in our ears, feed us with Himself. The entire Old and

New Testament reveal and proclaim an intimate God desiring intimacy with us, His people. The homily, when created as an act of cooperation with the Holy Spirit, who intimately hovers from the very beginning over creation,[9] will always reflect some level of this deep connection. "Communication is more than the expression of ideas and the indication of emotion. At its most profound level it is the giving of self in love."[10]

At some point, in order to be able do this, you may well have to dig more deeply into your own woundedness. Poet David Whyte speaks of the "*well* of grief," the "place we cannot breathe," and the finding of the "source from which we drink."[11] That's where you will find a deeper understanding and compassion that needs to be poured into the homily. Not that you share your inner wounds with your parishioners, but that you draw from that deep well of experience, its reservoir of grace and wisdom.

---

[9] Genesis 1:2

[10] *"Communio Et Progressio"* On the Means of Social Communication, Part 1, 11. Second Vatican Council, May 23, 1971.

[11] David Whyte, *Close to Home*, Ish River Productions, CD, 1992.

Returning to the Light in the Homily

Once you make the choice in your homily to enter deep waters with your congregation, you have a responsibility to bring your listeners safely back to the shore. It was a common practice of psychological self-awareness encounter groups in the 1960s and 1970s to open people's hearts through interpersonal confrontation tactics to their personal tragedies and deep inner despair and then leave them there, often with tragic personal consequences. Your homily can gently look at the darkness of fallen human nature and tragedies in human life as long as you eventually bring your listeners into the hope of the Resurrection. You can ask the dark questions if you can offer the answers of hope, grace, and light. You can do open heart surgery only if you are prepared to heal the heart and close it back up in order that it might once again pump the liquid of life through your patient. Be very careful in your homily touching upon the extremely tragic issues of abortion, adultery, divorce, drug addiction, sexual deviations, the death of children, and suicide. Keep in mind that your audience is required to go to Mass; therefore, your homily is not like a lecture that they have chosen to attend. They are at your mercy; be respectful of the unseen deep wounds that many carry. "Nearly all parish communities include women and men who have been harmed emotionally and spiritually by an abortion experience. While reminding the community of the beauty and

sacredness of human life, the homilist should always emphasize God's infinite mercy for all sinners, including those suffering after an abortion. Like the woman at the well, such individuals need to be invited to approach the Church without
fear, in order to receive God's forgiveness and healing
grace."[12] (Later on, we will look specifically at the Pro-Life
homily and how the tragedy of abortion can be handled appropriately in homily.)

Offer light without making light of the journey. The
heart's movement from darkness to light, unforgiveness to
forgiveness, despair to hope, sickness to wholeness, and sorrow to joy, can be a tumultuous, difficult, and complicated
journey for many. Never give the impression that inner healing is simple, easy, or effortless.

---

[12] *Preaching the Mystery of Faith: The Sunday Homily,* Committee on Clergy, Consecrated Life, and Vocations, USCCB approved 2012.

Chapter 7

The Closer

Ending the Homily-The Landing

The homily is over; you have said all that needs to be said; the homiletic flight is finished, but you just can't figure out how to land the plane. You are stuck at the pulpit waiting for some curtain to come down and end it. But that's not happening, so you scramble for some *ad hoc* way to close up shop in hopes that no one will notice. Everyone notices a bumpy misguided plane landing, and no one misses the actor stuck on stage. So, with these two dismal images in mind, let's take a look at several ways in which you should NOT end a homily:

The Prayer. The entire Mass is a prayer in which the Church in her wisdom has carefully worded and set prayers in their proper place and now you decide to throw in an extra one for good measure because you can't properly end your homily. These scripted get-me-out-of-here prayers make your voice go into the same high-speed voice mode that we have discussed earlier concerning other forms of quotations. To make matters worse, because you are about to leave the pulpit, your voice also tends to go into mumble mode.

Mumbling *"Let the words of my mouth and the meditation of our hearts, be acceptable in thy sight oh Lord"* does not help your homily but serves to lose your final strong landing statement. If your homily blesses us there will be no need for a *God bless you!* in order to land.

The Sour Note. If your homily has discussed difficulties in morality, difficulties in the world, difficulties in our journey to Christ, please do not end your homily on a sour or sad note. Remember inspiration! Never allow your homily, no matter how dark the topic, to get mired in sin, hopelessness, death, and darkness. Please complete your homily in virtue, hope, in the immeasurable availability of grace, and in the light of Resurrection.

The Hebrew. If you are the kind of personality that can end with a dynamic *Amen! Can I hear an Amen?!* and can get a strong response from your congregation, by all means indulge in our beloved Hebrew *Amen!* However, please refrain from a mumbled furtive ~*amen*~ to get yourself away from the pulpit. This sad weaseling ~*amen*~ serves only to undermine even more your lack of understanding of a final strong landing for your homily and confuses your congregation. It says that even you are not sure that your homily is worthy of a true and substantial Amen!

The Apology. If your homily has gone on a bit longer than usual, please don't apologize as a means of ending your homily and getting yourself away from the pulpit. You either gave a great homily even though longer than usual in which case there is no reason to apologize, or you rambled on and on in which case there is no point in bringing that to our attention as we are already well aware, and your apology doesn't really help matters.

The Thank You. If and only if your homily is really boring and miserable should you thank your listeners for having to listen to you. Otherwise, they should be thanking you. A *thank you* invites at least an internal return comment of *you're welcome* and now you have a little mini dialogue commencing at the end of your homily that doesn't belong in the Mass. Learn to end your homily on a proper note that wraps up the entire package properly, without niceties that are more proper to other settings such as lectures.

The Take-off and the Landing, the beginning and the end, are the parentheses that surround your homily; they are the tail ends of the thread that you have hopefully woven through your homily, and which you will now use to cinch it tight. It is often a good idea to plan and even memorize your landing, so that you can indeed land both gracefully and strongly. If you could only speak one sentence for your homily, this should usually be it. This sentence can be a statement; this sentence can be a question, for example: *Would that you and I hope never to deny Jesus again! Will you and I hope never to deny Jesus again?! Never forget that Jesus, the Good Shepherd carries each of us in His loving arms! Can we try to remember this week, that Jesus carries each of us in His loving arms?!* Notice that these are strong emphasized statements that hold clarity, vision, and promise. Information, formation, inspiration.

If your homily contained one primary point and several subpoints, your landing should emphasize once again your, let's say, three points. For example: *During these 40 days of Lent let us find new ways to come closer to Jesus through prayer, fasting, and giving to the poor. Or: During this season of Advent may we come to know God's presence, our presence to others in need, and lastly, the presents under the tree.*

The strong and graceful landing reminds us that you really believe what you have just told us in the homily. It doesn't leave us with the impression that you ran out of steam, have a lack of conviction, or are tired of addressing us. Your energy gives us energy, your confidence gives us confidence, your hope gives us hope; we are one Body, one Body in Christ. Do not confuse strong humility with weak arrogance. Strong humility means that you have confidence in your homily; it is a sense of certainty that you claim through grace and prayer.

Length of the Homily

With the homily take-off and landing in mind, it is only natural that one would question the length of the flight itself. It has been attributed to Abraham Lincoln that when asked how long a man's legs should be, he responded "Long enough to reach from his body to the ground."[1] It would do you well to keep this quote in mind. Your homily should be no longer than necessary to get your point across while offering information, formation, and inspiration without overwhelming those listening. I have heard great homilies that were under four minutes and some that pushed twenty minutes or more. Keep in mind that the first home of the homily is within the Mass itself, therefore the homily should never usurp the Mass like an unruly child in the home. The homily must keep in check a balance between the Liturgy of the Word and the Liturgy of the Eucharist; it cannot run on like a sermon or lecture may.

One of my favorite permanent-deacon-in-training was a wonderful gentleman named Brian. He was at first very shy, introverted, and lacked confidence, and was very unaware of the improvement he was making each week. One evening he didn't show up for class at all, even though his car was in the parking lot. We sent out search signals and finally located

---

[1] Thomas Lowry, *Personal Reminiscences of Abraham Lincoln*, (London: Chiswick Press, 1910), p. 23.

him in the library bemoaning his homily. He said it was un-finished; I told him to get to class! Finally, as the last practice homily for the night, Brian moved miserably and very reluc-tantly to the podium. I think we were all expecting a mess of a homily, but from his heart Brian proceeded to pour the au-thentic love, mercy, and beauty of God upon us. There was complete silence in the room; tears flowed down my face. When he ended, he looked up and said, "I'm sorry, that's all I've got; I didn't finish it." Through tears I asked Brian, "What more did you want the Holy Spirit to give you?!" His practice homily was less than five minutes long and changed our lives.

Listen to the instruction of the Holy Spirit, your heart, and your intellect, as well as your familiarity with the audi-ence to whom you speak, in determining the length of your homily. Consider also the words of Pope Benedict XVI: "The time spent by a priest in prayer and listening to Scripture is never time lost to pastoral care or time withheld from others. People sense whether the work and words of their pastor spring from prayer or are fabricated at his desk."[2] Remember as well, the homily's home within the Mass, and the homes to which it is destined: the mind and life of the listener. Learn when to continue and learn when to stop. How long should

---

[2] Pope Benedict XVI, *A New Song for the Lord* (Chestnut Ridge, NY: Crossroad Publishing, 1996), pp.46-47.

a particular homily be? Long enough to reach from the body to the ground, for the journey of faith.

Bear in mind that the homily "is a distinctive genre, since it is preaching situated within the framework of a liturgical celebration; hence it should be brief and avoid taking on the semblance of a speech or a lecture. A preacher may be able to hold the attention of his listeners for a whole hour, but in this case his words become more important than the celebration of faith. If the homily goes on too long, it will affect two characteristic elements of the liturgical celebration: its balance and its rhythm."[3]

A final note on homily length concerning daily Mass homilies: please keep in mind that many of your faithful daily communicants are squeezing Mass into their schedule before rushing off to work in the morning or on their lunch hour from work. Therefore, your homily should be short and to the point. Save your longer thoughts for morning or afternoon discussion groups for the unemployed or retired folks that attend daily Mass and whose schedules are more flexible.

---

[3] *Evangelii Gaudium*, 138.

Chapter 8

Unique Moments

Blunders, Blasts, and Boo-Boos during the Homily

Lots of unexpected things can happen during the homily. Things can happen to you, your parishioners, and in the environment. The possibility of some of these can be foreseen and planned for ahead of time so that when they happen their effect while not entirely eradicated can be mitigated. Let's take a look at several common issues:

Dropping the pages, notes, index cards of your homily: Always number your note pages. It's that simple. Assume that eventually you will drop them, and they will get all mixed up. I just recently watched a priest spend several minutes fumbling and apologizing while scrambling to rearrange in proper order his unnumbered homiletic notes.

Bungling or forgetting a line of your homily: Sooner or later even the best of speakers bungles or botches up a word, sentence, or concept within the homily. Rule of thumb: never apologize, just move on with the correct words. Let your face apologize, not your voice. Spoken apologies tend to illicit spoken or thought responses from your audience, which you do not want because they interfere even more with the flow of the homily. Remember that your audience has no idea what you plan to say, so while you know the bungle, chances are that they are often unaware.

Losing your train of thought: It happens. Be silent and think. Close your eyes, breathe, pray if necessary. As above, do not apologize. Apologies when speaking only serve to make your audience more uncomfortable, and you look worse. In life, apologies are a sign of strength; in speaking presentations they are a sign of weakness.

The Ringing Cell Phone: Rule of thumb—1 ring gets ignored, 2 rings get a smile and a raised eyebrow, and 3 rings gets a comment such as *Perhaps God is calling?!* Or *I hope that's not my mother-in-law!* This gets a laugh, allows the person time to dig through their belongings and silence the phone, and shows that you can handle an interruption with grace and charm.

The Crying Baby: As with the cell phone there is the 1, 2, and 3 second crying or screaming rules of thumb. Unless, extremely loud, the first squawk gets ignored, then a smile, then a charming comment while the parent makes an exit. Do not attempt to shriek or holler the homily over a screaming child; I've seen this attempted, and the child always wins that competition, much to everyone's chagrin. Wait, and if necessary, suggest the cry room or a walk outside.

Fire Trucks, Ambulances, and Miscellaneous External Disruption: If it sounds like all hell is breaking loose outside the church walls, please do not ignore it. Stop, wait, allow the commotion to pass. Do not attempt to yell or shout over the disturbance. Acknowledge it, perhaps a minor comment concerning it, no apologies for it, and then regroup your homiletic moment with a simple *There now, let us continue our thoughts.*

Medical Emergencies Within the Church: Do not continue your homily if there is a medical emergency within the congregation or at the altar. Ascertain that 911 has been called, allow silence, if necessary, for several moments. Do not continue the homily as though oblivious to a serious matter. If emergency medical personnel must take someone out on a stretcher, please just wait quietly. Once the stricken person is out of the church proper, regroup your congregation with a brief word of concern or prayer *We pray for our friend as we continue with a few more thoughts here.*

The Slamming door, The Banging book, The Crashing kneeler: Loud noises happen. Sometimes they make you or your parishioners jump out of their skin; do not attempt to ignore a noise of great magnitude. If everyone has jumped or cringed, plan a way to make light of it. *Well, perhaps God is trying to wake us all up this morning!* This will get light laughter and let the embarrassed offender off the hook. On the other hand, loud bodily noises such as burps, gas, and associated stomach rumblings are best ignored, unless it is your stomach grumbling at the podium.

Special Occasion Homilies

The Family or Children's Mass Homily

There is always the temptation to dumb down the homily for children, which is far different from simplifying the homily. Children are persons, not unintelligent beings in small bodies. Children hate being talked down to and only the very youngest of children tolerate being cutely baby-talked to. Years ago, so fed up with being talked down to in a teen religion class, my 13-year-old son, when asked *What does Emmanuel mean?* Answered: *A pamphlet that comes with a major appliance.* Young children as well as older teenagers desire to be challenged and engaged, so do not placate with embarrassing platitudes.

That being said, there are some clear things not to address in a general Family Mass. Avoid discussions of murder, terrorist activity, abortion, and other grave evils in the world at large. You may think this is obvious, but I have heard some horrific Family Mass homilies. In other words, respect the level of innocence to which you speak and attend to it.

If a child in the parish has given you something, such as a crayon drawing, and you wish to use this little gift as a prop within your homily at the Family Mass, please be attentive to what it is, and any connotations associated with it. After the great sorrow of the recent Scandal, you cannot be too vigilant. For example, if you have a drawing of the child's house, car, family pet, well that's great. But one seminarian I was teaching was given a drawing of little Sally's bedroom and decided to use that in his practice homily. No! Please, no mention of children in connection with bedrooms, bathrooms, or being alone with a child; nothing even mildly intimate regarding a child should ever be mentioned in a homily. This includes one-on-one talks, encounters, playing. If there ever was a time of innocence regarding these matters, it is over now and gone. Be vigilant. Children are not to be avoided but encountered in transparent situations that allow warmth and closeness, while keeping everyone safe.

Children love props, so if you are ever considering using a prop, the Children's Mass is a great place to try one out. That being said, they like awesome props, not dumb ones. They are looking for the *cool* factor and are less forgiving than adults when it comes to a dumb prop; they will more clearly associate you with the prop. I saw one of my deacons charm a group of young teens using only his cell phone as a prop for prayer, learning to talk with God as easily as you chat with your friends. It worked. But he had the personality to go with the prop. You are never separate from your prop; remember that. (See the earlier section on Props.)

Two Unique Homily Situations

"We know, too, that at certain moments in the liturgical year, such as Christmas or Easter, the assembly will likely include many Catholics who participate only occasionally in the Church's liturgy. Although not in the context of Sunday worship, similar pastoral opportunities are present at weddings or funerals, when family members who may have strayed from the practice of their faith are present at these moments of family joy and sorrow. This is obviously not the time to chide such Catholics for their absence. Rather, the homilist should use the beauty of the liturgy and the contents of the homily to open the Scriptures, to make a gracious and thoughtful connection to the meaning of Christian faith in the world today, and to invite back those who have lost contact with the Church. This is precisely the rationale of the call for a New Evangelization of those Catholics who, for whatever reason, have drifted away from their spiritual home. Through the prayerful celebration of the Eucharistic ritual and through the graceful and respectful proclamation of the word, all are invited to be aware of their deepest spiritual and human longings and to immerse themselves again in the mystery of Christ present in the Eucharist, who alone is able to quench their deepest spiritual thirst."[1]

The Wedding Homily and the Funeral Homily are unique in that they both have something very unusual in common: the presence, often, of completely *unchurched* people as well as many *dechurched people*. By completely *unchurched* I refer to people who have perhaps never set foot in a church before, were never baptized, were not as children brought up in any kind of religious tradition, and who have never even considered organized religion in any way pertinent to their life. By *dechurched people* I refer to those who for one reason or another have not darkened the door of a church or ecclesial community for many years, perhaps since they were teenagers, or since the divorce, or since the abortion. But now these *un* and *de churched* folks have a dear friend who is getting married or who has died, and here at long last they find themselves back in the pew. For the former group, this may be the only homily they ever hear in their lifetime; for the latter, this may be the only homily that might, by the grace of God, return them to the fold. "In our day many Catholics have drifted away from active participation in the Church and are in need themselves of hearing

---

[1] *Preaching the Mystery of Faith: The Sunday Homily*, Committee on Clergy, Consecrated Life, and Vocations, USCCB approved 2012.

again the Gospel of Jesus Christ and of recommitting them-selves to discipleship...In order to awaken this hunger and thirst for the word of God in our time, we need to renew our preaching with lively faith, firm conviction, and joyful wit-ness."[2]

If you are not mindful of these two groups in the prepa-ration of your homily, you ignore two of the greatest possi-bilities for evangelization that exist. Many a funeral homily focuses on the dead guy and many a wedding homily focuses on the bride and groom, none of whom are in any position to appreciate the homily. The former is, well, dead, and the latter two are focused on the reception, has the cake arrived intact? Anything of importance that you wanted to say to these two should have been said, please God, well before the wedding. However, your listeners are the *dearly beloved* of the couple or of the deceased; they are a captive audience to your homily, the only one they may ever hear. What do you have to tell them of the love of God the Father, the mercy of His Son Jesus Christ, the grace poured out through His Mother Mary, and the ever-present hope of the Holy Spirit?! What can you offer them this day that might reach their hearts? <u>Do not underestimate the opportunity of the funeral and wedding Mass to reach the *unchurched* and the *de-*</u>

---

[2] *Preaching the Mystery of Faith: The Sunday Homily,* Com-mittee on Clergy, Consecrated Life, and Vocations, USCCB ap-proved 2012.

churched; this opportunity for you and for them may never come again.

Now let's take a look at what other things need to be included in these two unique Masses:

The Funeral Homily

The Funeral homily is often confused with a Beatification or Canonization homily, and it is important that this confusion not happen. Unless you can hear chanting outside the church walls of _Santo Subito!_ it is best to assume that the deceased is not a saint, and therefore is still in need of the prayers of the faithful; therefore, you may need to include a very brief but essential understanding of the gift of purgatory. _The souls of the just are in the hands of God_ and by the hope of grace, the unjust might, we pray, be in purgatory. Hell is usually best not mentioned at a funeral homily, however tempting. It is better to make clear that "In the presence of Christ, who is Truth itself, the truth of each man's relationship with God will be laid bare. The Last Judgment will reveal even to its furthest consequences the good each person has done or failed to do during his earthly life...The message of the Last Judgment calls men to conversion while God is still giving them 'the acceptable time' . . .The Church prays that no one should be lost: "Lord, let me never be parted from you." If it is true that no one can save himself, it is also true that God "desires all men to be saved," and that for him 'all things are possible.'"[3]

Never use the funeral homily as a means to confuse theology in an effort to comfort the bereaved, and therefore do not resort to the false idea that the deceased has *become an angel or received wings* or any other such theological whimsy. Especially at the funeral of a child, it is important that the bereaved understand that the little one is a child of God and in His care.

Keep always in mind that immortality is found only in Jesus Christ. Therefore, "beware of offering secular comfort. For instance, it may be tempting to posit for the dead person a pseudo-immortality, suggesting that the deceased one lives on in his or her works and thoughts and lasting achievements, or in our memories, or in his or her descendants."[4]

The immediate family of the deceased are to be consoled *by name*. This includes the spouse (significant other), parents, children, siblings, and grandparents, if present. Get the names, write them down, and if at all possible, be able to identify them. Jesus calls us by name, consoles us by name, embraces us by name.

The homily is not the eulogy. The Church has asked that the eulogy be given at the reception for the deceased, rather

---

[3] *Catechism of the Catholic Church*, 1039, 1041, 1058.

[4] Reginald H. Fuller, Daniel Westberg, *Preaching the Lectionary*, 3rd edition (Collegeville, MN: Liturgical Press, 2006), p. 574.

than as part of the Mass. Therefore, limit comments on the life of the deceased to a few brief poignant, funny, or joyful remarks, and then, allow the homily to point to the mercy of our Lord Jesus Christ, and consolation of the Holy Spirit for both the deceased and those left behind in this time of great sorrow: A theme of consolation in the desolation, a theme of hope.

Not all deaths are equal. The loss of a baby or child, the suicide of a teenager, the demise of a young parent to cancer or a car accident are radically different than the passing of the elderly grandparent who lived a good life and died a happy death. Be mindful of the *kind of death* you are dealing with in this funeral homily for this family.

Not all grieving is equal. Not all of the family members, or the family-in-laws, may be in favor of this funeral Mass; some may, in fact, be quite hostile to it. There may be many conflicting emotions of which you may be aware or may not be aware at this funeral; tread carefully, assume nothing. Not everyone is there because they loved the deceased; some are there out of obligation, social pressure, or to console some-one who did love the person whom they hated. The deceased may have been a loving husband and father or, on the other hand, a miserable abusive alcoholic to whom everyone is glad to bid *adieu*.

There may be regrets of many kinds, things said that ought not to have been said, as well as things left unsaid that ought to have been said. Be mindful of the *kind of grief* you are dealing with in this funeral homily for this family. Emotions run rampant at funerals; be careful what you say. On the other hand, truly grieving hearts are often wide open to receive grace. So be care-full what you say.

There is an old tombstone saying that reads *Remember me as you pass by/As you are now, so once was I/As I am now, so you shall be/Prepare for death and follow me*. This is a good thing to keep in mind within the funeral homily, the understanding that we all die. We are in this mortal boat together, but so is Jesus, who radically changed death forever by his Resurrection and Who offers immortality. This is the God who loves you now, right now, as you are; come home to Jesus today, for no other reason than that you are loved. *In this Great Holy Person of Love is our preparation for death.* That is the core of the funeral homily. Not the deceased, but the merciful and bountiful love of God: Father, Son, and Holy Spirit. (Please see related topic above on the *unchurched* and *dechurched* at the funeral Mass.)

Lastly, allow me to refer you once again to the homily of Father Paul Scalia, priest, and son of the late US Supreme Court Justice Antonin Scalia, at his father's funeral Mass on February 20, 2016. Readily available on the internet, this homily is the height of perfection of a funeral homily, having within it all the essential elements referred to above combined with Fr. Scalia's eloquence of delivery.

The Wedding Homily

The wedding homily needs to mention the three fundamental aspects of Catholic marriage: Faithful unity of one man and one woman, indissolubility until death, and openness to life/children. Needless to say, all three of these pillars of marriage ought to have been discussed with the couple being married long before they now appear before you at the altar. If you have neglected to discuss one or the other, the wedding homily is certainly not the time or place to suddenly spring on them, for example, the Church's stand on contraception. The wedding homily is NOT marriage preparation or marriage counseling. However, "in the face of widespread confusion in the sphere of affectivity, and the rise of ways of thinking which trivialize the human body and sexual differentiation, the word of God re-affirms the original goodness of the human being, created as man and woman and called to a love which is faithful, reciprocal and fruitful"[5] in a gentle, but clear message within the wedding homily.

The wedding homily needs to make clear that marriage in the Church is a Sacrament and as such it bestows grace; it is not merely a legal contract. Referring always to the bride and groom by name, the homily is a moment to call the couple, as well as the entire congregation, present back into the

---

[5] *Verbum Domini*, 85.

possibility of holiness that God bestows by grace, participation in His Life.

The wedding homily needs to make clear that no matter what state of life one is in, be it single, married, divorced, lay person, religious, or clergy, everyone is called to holiness. No matter if your ship is sailing well with sails full, or your life has become shipwrecked by misfortune, misadventure, or human bad choices, still there is the universal call to holiness and a return to a loving God. Many people at this wedding have shipwrecked marriages and feel that their spiritual life is over and done with. The wedding homily may be the only opportunity to call them home, invite them back into the life of the Church. Don't fail to do so!

There are many reasons that marriages fail but one reason stands out as a primary fundamental reason that most marriages fail: *Unforgiveness.* It is essential that the wedding homily mention the *importance of forgiveness* and the *human inability to forgive,* over the course of a lifetime, without the continued grace of the Sacraments, especially the Eucharist and Reconciliation. "Marriage is a ministry of offense...If you cannot forgive, then do not marry. When you hear people celebrating 30, 40, 50 years of togetherness, they are celebrating forgiveness."[6]

----

[6] Wedding Homily by Fr. Hughes Sundeme, Ghana; printed in *Aleteia* article by Tom Hoppes, May 2, 2022.

Remember that this may be the one and only opportunity to extend an invitation to the *unchurched* people as well as the *dechurched people* to enter into, or back into, the life of God. Remember that beauty, followed by goodness and truth, are the primary attractors to the human person. Weddings are by their very nature beautiful. We all see the promise of new beginnings, new life, innocence, loveliness, in the midst of a difficult world. Weddings (and baptisms!) literally sparkle with promise and hope and love! Tap into that visual palpable joy, and save the harder unbridled truths for another day, when grace has opened the mind and heart to hear truth and bear truth. Be gentle and kind with the shipwrecked in the wedding congregation. They are so afraid and need to hear the beautiful words of Christ: *Be not afraid.* Come home prodigal child.

The Pro-Life Homily

The Pro-Life homily at a Mass being said <u>primarily for the cause of Pro-Life</u> or for the lives of the preborn or those who have been aborted or for those who have engaged on one level or another in this grave matter is the one time where you can speak with greater openness on the topic of abortion. The primary reason for this is because people are expecting it. You will not take anyone unawares. This does not mean that you can be insensitive to those who are present who may deeply regret their abortions. Remembering, once again, that the homily is part of the Mass, this is no time for name calling, blaming, politicking, hurting. It is a time to uphold life, reach out for the purpose of healing and reconciliation, offer a return to grace. One can denounce Satan and all his evil works without calling anyone in the congregation present a murderer of children.

Remember that the homily, every homily, is meant to bring together the tripod of information, formation, and inspiration that can be brought from the Home of the Mass to the Home of the Intellect to the Home of the Heart, such that it can be implemented in daily life. No one should ever be traumatized by a homily, and this includes a homily about the most horrible and sorrowful of grave matters, abortion.

Highly recommended for anyone intending to preach on this painful topic is my ten-hour seminar on *Understanding Abortion*, based on the book of the same title, which was given at Holy Apostles College and Seminary for seminarians, religious sisters, and professors that is available on the internet free of charge. This is easily accessed through my website at https://www.kikilatimer.com/abortion. Furthermore, the book itself goes into far more detail, and will also help you "clarify your own position, be able to articulate it clearly, and defend it when challenged."[7]

---

[7] Stephen D. Schwarz with Kiki Latimer, *Understanding Abortion- From Mixed Feelings to Rational Thought* (Idaho Falls, ID: Lexington Books, 2012), p. 4.

The Visiting Mission Homily

The mission homily often given by visiting priests from various religious orders for the purpose of promoting their mission work throughout the world deserves a quick moment of instruction primarily because the work they do is so important, and the objective of their homily is usually both to teach and raise funds in order to continue their work. Keep information to a minimum. Stick with a few of your most poignant personal stories that delight and touch the heart and hold back on monotonous statistics that we cannot remember and can google if we really need to know. Tell us about that one little child that made it all worthwhile rather than a statistic of the thousands you have served over the years. Paint a verbal picture of a memory that really matters to you and allow that memory to take root in our hearts. Look for stories that are funny, precious, heart wrenching, hopeful, stories that assure us that we too can make a difference in the world by our involvement, prayers, and resources.

Chapter 9

The Final Home of the Homily

Our entire focus has so far concerned the role of the homilist for the people of God. We have focused on the skills and preparations necessary for the homilist to put out into the deep. He must first and foremost recognize the Home of the homily within the Mass itself; the homily must assume its proper sacred role within the Mass. We have looked at ways in which the homily must then take up residence in the Home of the Intellect; therefore, the homily must be under-standable, simple, and coherent. Then the homily must move on to the Home of the Heart of the listener, touching the deep reservoir of love for the good. For we understand that it is the heart in union with the intellect, far more than the intellect alone that usually moves the will. We have seen the importance of the homilist as shepherd understanding his sheep, speaking personally to them, and knowing them, their world, their needs. There is much work to be done by our priests and deacons!

So, we have, in essence, placed the entire burden of the homily onto the shoulders of the homilist, and to many this seems hardly fair! What of the listeners, the people of God, the parishioners, the laity? Do they bear no responsibility? It is a fair question and one to which the Church has responded with clear answers.

The final Home for the homily is in the movement of the Will of individuals; this is the domain of the domestic Church, the individual, familial, and communal lives of those who hear the homily. They, the people of God, must take the homily home. It is not enough to hear, understand, and love the homily; one must, finally, <u>do</u> the homily, <u>act</u> the homily, <u>work</u> the homily. For the homily without works is homeless, as "faith without works is dead."[1]

Furthermore, the "church has not been really founded, and is not yet fully alive, nor is it a perfect sign of Christ among men, unless there is a laity worthy of the name working along with the hierarchy... Their main duty, whether they are men or women, is the witness which they are bound to bear to Christ by their life and works in the home, in their social milieu, and in their own professional circle... Let the clergy highly esteem the arduous apostolate of the laity. Let them train the laity to become conscious of the responsibility which they as members of Christ have for all men."[2]

The homily is part of the continuous training of both the homilist and the laity in which together they might put out into the deep, be fed, and find a final working *Home for the Homily* in everyday life.

---

[1] NRSVCE James 2:26.
[2] *Ad Gentes*, 21.

In Conclusion

Instruct the Intellect
Move the Affections
Sway the Will

These concepts gleaned from the *Summa Theologica* of St. Thomas Aquinas have been dissected for practical application in homily in these preceding pages. Here we have hopefully encountered a deeper understanding of the role of both the intellect and the heart in the movement of the will toward the good. Comprehending the journey of the homily is essential for the homilist: from the homily's initial home in the Mass, to that of the intellect and then the heart of the listener before it comes to its final home in the acting will within life of the individual. This requires that the homilist have faith, humility, discernment, knowledge, wisdom, as well as great skill. Peter had all of these when he called Jesus "Master" and put out into the deep and lowered his nets for a catch. That day, Jesus declared that Peter would become a "fisher of men" and indeed he did. You too, with skill in *The Sacred Art of Homiletics* may with perseverance, great faith, and grace, follow our beloved St. Peter and put out into the deep, where in the Sacred context of the Mass, through the mind, heart and will of the listener, the homily will be brought home.

Recommended Resources

- *Ad Gentes*
- *Benedictus Day by Day with Pope Benedict XVI* Pope Benedict XVI
- Catechism of the Catholic Church
- *Communio Et Progressio* On the Means of Social Communication
- *Dei Verbum*
- *Evangelii Gaudium*
- *For Real? Christ's Christ's Presence in the Eucharist* – Dcn. Dennis Lambert
- *Forming Consciences for Faithful Citizenship - Part I - The U.S. Bishops' Reflection on Catholic Teaching and Political Life*
- *Fulfilled in Your Hearing*
- *Homiletic Directory* Congregation for Divine Worship
- *How to Make Homilies Better, Briefer, Bolder* Alfred McBride
- *Homily Abuse*, Lingayen-Dagupan Archbishop Socrates Villegas at the Cathedral of Lingayen-Dagupan, April 2, 2015.
- *Lumen Gentium*
- *Preaching the Lectionary* Reginald H. Fuller, Daniel Westberg

- *Preaching the Mystery of Faith: The Sunday Homily*
- *Silence the Mystery of Wholeness* Robert Sardello
- *Summa Theologica* St. Thomas Aquinas
- *The Art of Listening to Young People,* Amoris Christi
- *Theology As Prayer: A Primer for the Diocesan Priest* Walter R. Oxley, John P. Cush
- *Understanding Abortion: From Mixed Feelings to Rational Thought* Stephen Schwarz, Kiki Latimer
- *Verbum Domini*

www.ingramcontent.com/pod-product-compliance
Lightning Source LLC
Chambersburg PA
CBHW052129270326
41930CB00012B/2813